MW01489636

100 MYSTERIES OF PUBERTY FOR GIRLS

A Guide for Teens with Answers to Their Intimate Questions About Sex, Love, Friendship, Addictions, Health, Internet, and More

Magda Pabst

Table of Contents

About Magda Pabst

My name is Magda Pabst, and I am a passionate educator specializing in child and adolescent development. My mission is to support parents and teachers in guiding children and students in a fun, engaging, and educational way.

Throughout my career, I have worked extensively on topics such as emotional development, impulse control, anger management, ADHD, and adolescent challenges.

When I'm not immersed in new educational projects or writing specialized content, I enjoy spending time in nature and with my children. My goal is to help parents and teachers create the best possible environment for young minds and hearts to flourish—so they can explore the world with confidence and empathy.

I firmly believe that even the smallest gestures can have a profound impact on the future of our children and students. That's why I sincerely hope my work helps parents and teachers build a better world for the next generation.

If you have any questions, feedback, or notice any errors in this book—which I will gladly correct—please feel free to reach out to me at m.pabst.en@booksgopublications.com. I'll get back to you as soon as possible.

I have written several books about children and teenagers, all available on Amazon. You can find more information about me and my books on my publisher's website: www.booksgopublications.com.

A Bonus for Parents

Dear parents,

Before you hand this book to your child, I have a special gift for you. But first—once you've downloaded it, stop reading! This book is for your son, unless you're tempted to take a sneak peek. From the next chapter onward, the entire book is meant for him and him alone. And if you, dear teen, happen to be reading this section, feel free to skip ahead to the introduction. Here's your gift:

A Free eBook: *Deciphering Puberty and Understanding Adolescent Behavior*

This eBook explores common adolescent behaviors that parents often struggle to understand. Gaining deeper insight into these behaviors will help you better support your child and strengthen your bond with her. This bonus is designed to help you become a more understanding parent and provide your child with the right guidance during these sometimes challenging years.

Download Your Free Bonus!

You can download your free bonus by scanning the following QR code with your smartphone:

Introduction

Do you feel like your body and mind are changing, but you're not exactly sure how? Do your parents seem more annoying than usual? Do you have a million questions swirling in your head? Don't worry—it's all part of growing up and transitioning into puberty! This is a time of big changes and lots of new things to learn. This book will help you understand what's happening to you and give you the confidence to navigate this phase of your life. Puberty can sometimes feel confusing or overwhelming, but it's also an exciting time. Your body changes, your emotions become more intense, and you start to see the world differently. The first thing I want you to know is that every girl experiences puberty in her own way and at her own pace. Some changes might happen earlier for you, while your friends might develop at a different rhythm. And that's perfectly okay! You should never feel "behind" or compare yourself to others—your body knows what it's doing. We'll talk more about this in just a moment. I hope this book will help you feel more comfortable with yourself and answer the intimate questions you may have about this important stage of your life.

Each chapter of this book focuses on a different aspect of puberty. Within each chapter, you'll find 10 "mysteries" (for a total of 100), which are essentially key things you need to know as you go through puberty. These are often the source of doubts, worries, or embarrassing questions for girls your age. For many of these "mysteries," you'll also find practical tips that you can apply in your daily life. After all, I want this book to be useful and fun for you! I know theory can be boring, and the last thing I want is to make you yawn. The 100 "mysteries" in this book are divided into 10 main themes:

1. **Body Changes.** You'll learn all about the physical transformations you'll experience, from breast growth to pimples, from body hair to your first period. Most importantly, you'll discover how to accept and embrace these inevitable changes.

2. **Physical, Mental, and Emotional Health.** You'll find tips on managing mood swings, stress, and anxiety while staying physically and mentally healthy. We'll also talk about the importance of a balanced diet and getting enough sleep.

3. **Sexuality.** You'll learn what sex is and how it happens. We'll also discuss topics like touching, masturbation, and how to have safe sex to prevent unwanted pregnancy and STIs (Sexually Transmitted Infections). I'll give you all the information you need to approach this part of life with confidence and peace of mind.

4. **Boys, Love, and Relationships.** You'll gain insight into relationships with boys, romance, respect, consent, and intimacy. We'll also talk about how to handle heartbreak, what makes a healthy relationship, and how to communicate effectively with your partner.

5. **Social Life and Friendships.** Friendships play a crucial role in your life, and you'll learn how to build and maintain strong, positive relationships. We'll also talk about bullying and how to recognize and avoid toxic friendships.

6. **School and Learning.** You'll get practical advice on handling school stress, managing exam anxiety, and staying motivated to study. We'll also discuss how to find a study method that works for you and the benefits of learning a new hobby, playing an instrument, or trying a sport.

7. **Addictions.** You'll learn about the dangers of addictions, including smoking, alcohol, drugs, social media overuse, and compulsive shopping. We'll discuss how to recognize warning signs, avoid risky behaviors, and break free from unhealthy habits.

8. **Internet, Social Media, and Technology.** The internet and social media can be both amazing and dangerous. We'll explore online safety, fake news, cyberbullying, and the impact of social media on self-esteem. I'll also give you practical tips on using technology in a healthy and balanced way.

9. **Independence and Responsibility.** You'll discover how to make independent decisions, manage money, and prepare for adulthood. We'll also discuss essential practical skills and the importance of helping others.

10. **Your Relationship with Your Parents.** You'll learn how to better understand your parents, communicate with them effectively, and resolve conflicts in a constructive way.

I'm here to help you navigate the sometimes wild waters of puberty with a direct, fun, and even slightly quirky approach. Get ready to learn everything you need to know about this incredible stage of life—and how to become a confident, empowered young woman. Buckle up, and let's go!

Chapter 1: 10 Mysteries About Changes in Your Body

During puberty, your body undergoes a series of strange—and sometimes even a little scary—transformations. These changes can feel confusing and may even make you uncomfortable at times. In this section, we'll take a deep dive into the physical changes that occur during puberty. My goal is to help you feel more comfortable with your evolving body, while also understanding and accepting these changes. As multiple scientific studies have shown, every girl experiences puberty at her own pace, following a unique timeline[1]. There's no single "normal" pathway that applies to everyone. Keeping that in mind, let's explore what happens to your body as puberty unfolds.

1. The Phases of Puberty

Puberty happens in different phases, though it's impossible to define clear-cut age groups for each stage. Remember, every girl develops at her own rhythm! However, I'll outline the general phases of puberty for girls, along with approximate ages for reference. Just keep in mind that these are only rough estimates—if your experience doesn't match these timelines exactly, there's no need to worry!

Phase 1: Around 7–8 Years Old

At this stage, your body begins preparing for puberty. Hormones like estrogen start increasing, but there are very few visible physical changes. You might notice a slight growth spurt and feel more emotional than usual, but on the outside, not much looks different yet.

---

[1] **Wheeler, M. (1991).** *Physical changes of puberty.* Endocrinology and Metabolism Clinics of North America, 20(1), 1-14.

Phase 2: Around 9–10 Years Old

Between the ages of 9 and 10, changes become more noticeable. One of the first signs is the appearance of breast buds (a stage called thelarche), which feel like small lumps under your nipples—this means your breasts are starting to develop. You may also notice the first pubic hairs appearing, which start out soft and light before becoming thicker and darker. Around this time, your height also begins to increase significantly.

Phase 3: Around 11–12 Years Old

By the time you're 11 or 12, puberty is in full swing. Your breasts continue growing, and hair starts appearing under your arms. Acne might make an entrance due to increased oil production from your sebaceous glands. Your skin may feel oilier, and you'll likely start sweating more—especially during physical activity. You'll also begin noticing a more mature body shape, with your hips widening and fat naturally accumulating in areas like your thighs, stomach, and buttocks.

Phase 4: Around 13–15 Years Old

Between the ages of 13 and 15, your body begins to stabilize. Your growth slows down, and your breasts settle into their more defined shape, although for some girls, breast development can continue until they are 19 or even 20 years old. Hair starts to spread more across your body, becoming thicker and more noticeable. This phase is also marked by the start of your menstrual cycle, known as menarche. Your first period signals the beginning of female fertility and often comes with premenstrual syndrome (PMS)—a set of uncomfortable symptoms that many girls experience in the days leading up to their period, such as abdominal cramps, bloating, breast tenderness, muscle aches, irritability, increased appetite, and anxiety. We'll talk more about this later, but for now, just know that getting your first period is an important milestone in your journey. It may feel strange or overwhelming at first, but it's a completely natural process that all women go through. Your first period is a sign that your body is officially transitioning into adulthood. Welcome to womanhood!

Differences Between Boys and Girls

When it comes to puberty, boys and girls don't exactly go through the same process—or at the same pace. Boys usually start puberty later than girls. They grow facial hair, develop deeper voices, and their reproductive systems begin producing sperm. Their bodies take on an adult shape later than girls do, so if the boys of your age seem smaller or more immature, that's totally normal... because they are!

Don't Compare Yourself to Others

Puberty is a personal and unique journey for every girl—kind of like a sack race, where everyone reaches the finish line at their own speed. There's no set rule for how fast or slow you should develop, so comparing yourself to your friends is pointless and will only cause unnecessary stress. Trust your body's natural rhythm and embrace the process. Everyone gets there in the end—so take your time, enjoy the ride, and don't let worry get in the way of this incredible transformation!

2. Height, Weight, Voice, and Body Hair

During puberty, it's completely normal to notice a rapid and sometimes sudden increase in your height. One day, your clothes fit perfectly, and the next, you might need an entirely new wardrobe! This growth spurt is common for many teenage girls, but it doesn't happen the same way for everyone. Some girls experience steady, gradual growth instead of a sudden jump in height. Once again, every girl grows at her own pace! As your height increases, your weight will naturally increase as well. Your body needs to build mass to support your new height and develop muscle. So don't panic if you see a few extra kilos on the scale during this time. Puberty is a phase of growth and transformation, not a time to obsess over weight. If you feel like you're gaining a bit too much, try paying attention to your eating habits and staying active, but don't stress about counting every single calorie. Maintaining a balanced diet and engaging in regular physical activity is enough. Avoid extreme diets—they can do more harm than good!

Another common change during puberty is the slight deepening of your voice. While girls' voices don't change as dramatically as boys' do, you might notice that your voice sounds a bit deeper or different than before. This happens because your larynx is growing, and hormones are playing their part. There's nothing to be embarrassed about—it's a natural part of development. If you feel self-conscious about it, just remember that your voice will stabilize over time. As you probably already know, puberty also brings new hair growth in different areas of your body, including your underarms, legs, and pubic region. Managing this hair is a personal choice. Many young women choose to remove it for aesthetic reasons or comfort. Here are some common options:

- **Shaving.** If you decide to shave, always use a clean, sharp razor and apply shaving cream or gel to prevent irritation. Never share razors with others to avoid infections.

- **Waxing.** Waxing removes hair at the root, providing longer-lasting results than shaving. You can do it at home with special kits or visit a professional esthetician. While waxing can be a little painful, it leaves the skin smooth for several days.

- **Depilatory creams.** These creams dissolve hair at the surface. They're easy to use, but may cause irritation in people with sensitive skin. Always follow the product instructions carefully.

- **Electric epilators.** These devices pluck hair from the root, similar to waxing. They provide long-lasting results, but can be a bit painful.

- **Laser and IPL (Intense Pulsed Light).** These treatments offer permanent or semi-permanent hair removal. They must be performed by professionals and require multiple sessions. If you're considering this option, research the pros and cons, and check with the clinic about the minimum recommended age for treatment.

For more delicate areas, such as facial hair (yes, it's completely normal to have some!), I recommend visiting a professional beauty salon at least for your first time. A specialist can help you find the best hair removal method for your skin type and preferences. Regardless of the method you choose, always moisturize your skin after waxing or shaving to avoid irritation and keep it soft. Avoid sun exposure immediately after hair removal, and always keep your tools clean to prevent infections. Most importantly, remember that the decision to remove body hair—or not—is entirely yours. Don't feel pressured to do it just because others are. Your body is going through a period of transition, and what matters most is that you feel comfortable and confident in your own skin.

3. The Female Reproductive System

Learning how your reproductive system works might not sound like the most exciting topic, but trust me—it's important. Later in this book, we'll discuss the more practical side, like how to use your sexual organs, which I'm sure will grab your attention. But for now, let's focus on understanding what your reproductive system is, how it functions, and why puberty is the stage where it becomes fully active. The female reproductive system consists of the ovaries, fallopian tubes, uterus, vagina, and vulva. Here's what each part does.

Ovaries

The ovaries are two small, almond-shaped glands located on either side of the uterus. Their main role is to produce eggs and release female hormones, such as estrogen and progesterone. Every month, as part of the menstrual cycle (which we'll talk about soon), one ovary releases an egg in a process called ovulation.

Fallopian Tubes

These are two thin, muscular tubes that connect the ovaries to the uterus. When an ovary releases an egg, it enters one of the fallopian tubes, where it may meet a sperm cell and become fertilized. This is where fertilization happens if sperm is present.

Uterus

The uterus is a hollow, pear-shaped organ located in the lower abdomen. Its main function is to house and nourish an embryo during pregnancy. The inner lining of the uterus, called the endometrium, thickens each month in preparation for a possible pregnancy. If fertilization doesn't occur, the endometrial lining is shed during menstruation.

Vagina

The vagina is a muscular canal that connects the uterus to the outside of the body. It serves several functions: it allows menstrual blood to leave the body, acts as the birth canal during childbirth, and serves as the receiving organ during sexual intercourse. Its ability to stretch and contract is essential for all these functions.

Vulva

The vulva includes the external parts of the female reproductive system, such as the labia majora, labia minora, clitoris, and urethra. Its main role is to protect the internal reproductive organs and help maintain proper hygiene through fluid secretion. Among these external structures, the clitoris plays a key role in female sexual pleasure. It is a small, highly sensitive erectile organ that, when stimulated, can produce intense sensations.

4. The Menstrual Cycle

The menstrual cycle is a natural process that begins when a girl reaches puberty. It is the body's way of preparing for a possible pregnancy and is an essential part of the female reproductive system. Understanding how the menstrual cycle works can help you better manage its symptoms and be more aware of what's happening in your body. The cycle starts on the first day of menstruation, which is marked by vaginal bleeding, and ends the day before the next period begins. On average, a menstrual cycle lasts about 28 days, but it can range anywhere from 21 to 35 days. Let's take a closer look at its different phases.

- **The Menstrual Phase.** This phase coincides with the days of menstruation, when bleeding occurs. The endometrium, which is the lining of the uterus, is shed and expelled through the vagina. This process, known as menstrual flow, typically lasts between 3 and 7 days.

- **The Follicular Phase.** This phase also begins on the first day of menstruation but lasts until ovulation, which happens roughly halfway through the cycle. During this phase, hormones stimulate the ovaries to develop follicles, each containing an egg. At the same time, rising estrogen levels thicken the endometrium, preparing it for the possible implantation of a fertilized egg.

- **Ovulation.** This occurs around the middle of the cycle. During ovulation, one of the follicles releases a mature egg, which travels through the fallopian tubes toward the uterus. This is the most fertile phase of the cycle, meaning it's the time when pregnancy is most likely to occur if sperm is present.

- **The Luteal Phase.** This phase follows ovulation and lasts about 14 days. After releasing the egg, the ruptured follicle transforms into a structure called the corpus luteum, which produces progesterone to maintain the uterine lining. If the egg is not fertilized, levels of estrogen and progesterone drop, causing the endometrium to break down and shed, marking the start of a new menstrual cycle.

Different Products to Manage Menstruation

I know—it's annoying. But there's no way around it: you have to manage your period, and luckily, there are plenty of products available to help. Here are some of the most commonly used options:

- **Pads.** These are the most widely used menstrual products. They are absorbent strips that stick to your underwear, designed to soak up menstrual flow. They're easy to use and come in different sizes and levels of absorbency.

- **Tampons.** These are small absorbent devices inserted into the vagina. They offer greater freedom of movement, making them ideal for sports or swimming, but they can take a little practice to use correctly.

- **Menstrual cups.** These are small, flexible silicone or rubber cups inserted into the vagina to collect menstrual fluid. Since they are reusable, they are a more eco-friendly and cost-effective option.

What Are Premenstrual Symptoms and How Can You Manage Them?

Premenstrual Syndrome (PMS) refers to the physical and emotional symptoms many women experience in the days leading up to their period. The intensity and duration of these symptoms vary from person to person, but the most common include abdominal cramps, muscle pain, headaches, back pain, bloating, nausea, mood swings, fatigue, irritability, breast tenderness, appetite changes, and acne. Sounds great, right? Especially when you realize that men will never have to go through this! Just kidding—PMS is a completely natural process, and while it can be annoying, it's something you can learn to manage. Fortunately, there are many ways to ease these symptoms. The best approach is to maintain a healthy lifestyle. Exercising regularly, eating a balanced diet, and staying hydrated can make a huge difference. Even a short daily walk can help boost your energy levels and reduce fatigue. Painkillers can help relieve muscle aches, headaches, and back pain. To reduce bloating, make sure to drink plenty of water and eat foods rich in potassium—such as bananas and spinach—to help balance your body's fluid levels. Magnesium supplements can also help with water retention and bloating.

If you experience fatigue, mood swings, or irritability, make sure you're getting enough sleep—at least eight hours per night. These are general tips, but if you struggle with severe pain or intense PMS, don't hesitate to consult a doctor who can recommend the right treatment for you. Another helpful habit is tracking your menstrual cycle. This can help you anticipate your period and manage symptoms more effectively. You can use a simple calendar or a cycle-tracking app (there are plenty of free ones available) to record your period days, symptoms, and any irregularities. Finally, don't be afraid to talk openly about menstruation with your parents, family members, or a doctor. If you experience very painful periods, excessive bleeding, or irregular cycles, it's important to consult a doctor to check for any underlying issues. Taking care of your health is always the top priority!

5. Breast Growth

One of the first changes girls notice during puberty is breast growth. The first sign is the appearance of small lumps under the nipples, known as breast buds. This stage, as mentioned earlier, is called thelarche. Breast development continues throughout adolescence and, for some girls, even until the age of 19 or 20. The size and shape of breasts depend on several factors, including genetics, body fat, and hormone levels. Some girls naturally develop larger breasts than others. Genetics play the biggest role—if the women in your family have larger breasts, there's a good chance you will too, and vice versa. However, breast growth is not a competition. There's no reason to compare yourself to other girls or feel self-conscious if your breasts are smaller. Beauty comes in all shapes and sizes, and your body—including your breasts—is perfect just the way it is (or rather, how it will be once puberty is complete). Learning to accept and love your body is essential for your emotional and mental well-being. As your breasts grow, you may reach the point where you need your first bra. A sports bra or a soft, wireless bra is usually a good place to start, as it provides support without feeling too restrictive.

Over time, you can try different styles, such as underwire or padded bras, and choose what makes you feel most comfortable. To find the right bra size, you'll need to take two measurements: the band size (the measurement around your ribcage, just under your breasts) and the bust size (the measurement around the fullest part of your breasts). In the U.S., band sizes are measured in inches and usually come in even numbers, like 30, 32, 34, 36, etc. The cup size is determined by subtracting the band size from the bust measurement—the difference corresponds to letters like A, B, C, D, etc.. For example, if your bust measures 34 inches and your band size is 32 inches, the difference is 2 inches, which means you'd typically wear a 32B. When trying on a bra, make sure the band fits snugly but comfortably and that the cups fully support your breasts without squeezing or leaving gaps. Since different brands fit differently, it's always a good idea to try on several styles to find the best fit for your body. Keep in mind that your bra size can change over time as your body develops, so it's important to check your measurements regularly and adjust your bra size as needed. Wearing a bra that fits well will help you feel more comfortable and confident as your body continues to change.

6. Sweat, Body Odor, and Personal Hygiene

Puberty comes with increased sweating—and sometimes, an unpleasant odor. This happens because your sweat glands become more active, especially in areas like your armpits, feet, and private parts. Sweat itself doesn't actually smell bad, but when it mixes with bacteria on your skin, it can produce a strong, unpleasant odor. Luckily, there are plenty of ways to stay clean, fresh, and odor-free throughout the day. Here's how:

- **Shower regularly.** Take a shower at least once a day, especially after exercising. Use a good antibacterial soap to remove odor-causing bacteria. Pay extra attention to washing your underarms, feet, and intimate areas.

- **Use deodorant or antiperspirant.** A good underarm deodorant will help mask odor, while an antiperspirant reduces the amount of sweat your body produces.

- **Stay fresh with perfume.** If you like, you can use a light perfume or body spray to smell good all day—but don't overdo it!

- **Bring a change of clothes.** If you know you'll be sweating a lot, having a fresh shirt or extra pair of socks on hand can make a huge difference.

- **Keep your underwear clean.** Always change your underwear at least once a day, and if it's hot or you're sweating a lot, twice a day is even better.

- **Wash and dry your feet and armpits thoroughly.** Keeping these areas clean and completely dry will help prevent both odor and bacteria buildup.

7. Pimples

Ah, the first pimples. Just when you thought puberty couldn't get any more complicated, these little breakouts show up to add another challenge.

Many teenagers—both boys and girls—experience acne during puberty, but it doesn't have to be a major source of stress, or worse, affect your self-esteem. The good news? There are plenty of effective ways to manage and treat acne today. Pimples appear because of hormonal changes that stimulate the skin's sebaceous glands to produce more sebum—a natural, oily substance. When excess sebum mixes with dead skin cells, it can clog pores, creating the perfect environment for acne-causing bacteria to thrive. The result? Pimples, blackheads, and sometimes even painful cysts. To keep acne under control, take good care of your skin. Wash your face twice a day with a gentle cleanser, and avoid touching or popping pimples—this can worsen inflammation and lead to scarring. For years, people believed that eating chocolate or sugary foods caused acne, but recent scientific studies have debunked this myth[2]. While a healthy diet is always beneficial, acne isn't just about what you eat—it's a real skin condition that requires proper care.

If your parents tell you to just "wait it out" because acne will go away on its own, they're not entirely right. Yes, even parents can be wrong! While some mild acne does clear up naturally, more severe cases need treatment to prevent scarring. If you're struggling with acne, insist on seeing a dermatologist. A doctor can determine what type of acne you have (there are different kinds, each requiring a different approach) and provide the right treatment—whether it's topical creams, medicated cleansers, or even oral medication. Taking action early can save your skin in the long run, so don't ignore acne—treat it!

8. Unexpected Changes During Puberty

In addition to all the changes we've already discussed, puberty brings several other transformations that might surprise you. Here are a few of them.

Brain

During adolescence, your brain undergoes a major restructuring in which many neuronal connections are either strengthened or eliminated. This

---

[2] **Fulton, J. E., Plewig, G., & Kligman, A. M. (1969).** *Effect of chocolate on acne vulgaris.* JAMA, 210(11), 2071-2074.

process, called synaptic pruning, is similar to trimming the dead branches of a tree to help it grow stronger. As a result, the way you think, learn, and manage emotions changes significantly. These brain changes also contribute to stronger emotions, impulsivity, and mood swings during puberty. But don't worry—once this phase is over, these "symptoms" will fade, or at least you'll get much better at managing them with experience.

Muscles

During puberty, you'll likely notice an increase in muscle mass, although this change is less pronounced in girls than in boys. This is because hormones like estrogen and testosterone stimulate muscle growth. Since girls naturally produce much lower levels of testosterone—the main hormone responsible for muscle development—their muscle growth tends to be more moderate. However, staying active is still important! Playing a sport 2–3 times a week can help build muscle, improve strength and endurance, and boost overall health. Activities like dance, volleyball, or other team sports are great not only for toning muscles but also for making new friends and having fun.

Lungs and Heart

Your lungs and heart also grow during puberty, improving lung capacity and endurance. You might find that physical activities feel easier, and your stamina increases over time.

Perception of the World

Finally, your perception of the world will also start to shift. You'll begin to see things from a more mature perspective, forming your own opinions and ideas with greater depth. Puberty is not just a period of physical changes—it's also a time of intellectual and emotional growth, helping you understand yourself and the world around you in a whole new way.

9. Embracing the Changes in Your Body

Accepting the physical, emotional, and intellectual changes that come with puberty is essential to navigating this phase with confidence and peace of mind. It's completely normal to feel a little confused or self-conscious about everything that's happening. Growth spurts, pimples, mood swings, breast development, body hair, the start of your menstrual cycle—it all seems to happen so fast. However, try to approach this stage with a positive mindset and a sense of curiosity about the changes taking place in your body and mind. Every transformation is a sign that you're growing up and entering a new chapter of your life. When you look in the mirror, remind yourself that these changes are part of the incredible journey of life. And most importantly, never forget that every girl experiences puberty in her own way and at her own pace. Your path is unique—so avoid comparing yourself to others and embrace your journey with confidence!

10. Body-Shaming

The physical changes that happen during puberty are sometimes mocked by others. This form of harassment, known as body-shaming, is a serious issue worldwide. Making fun of someone for their appearance or perceived imperfections is not only unfair but can also have devastating effects on their mental health and self-esteem. Never participate in this kind of behavior—not even toward people you don't like. Bullying related to body changes can take many forms, including teasing someone about their weight, height, breast development, or acne. Being mocked for something beyond your control can be incredibly hurtful and damaging to your self-confidence.

If someone makes fun of your physical appearance, remember that the issue is with them, not you. Bullies often lash out because of their own insecurities, using insults to make themselves feel better. Don't let their words define your self-worth. If you're being targeted, reach out to a trusted adult, such as a parent, teacher, or school counselor. They can offer guidance and help find a solution. Similarly, if you witness someone else being bullied, don't stay silent. Speak up and report the incident to an adult. Everyone deserves to be treated with respect, and standing up against bullying can make a real difference. We'll revisit the topic of bullying later in this book, but for now, just remember: you are not alone, and you deserve to feel confident and accepted just as you are.

Chapter 2: 10 Mysteries About Physical, Mental, and Emotional Health

Can you help me? If you're enjoying this book, I'd truly appreciate it if you could leave a review on Amazon by scanning the following QR code with your smartphone:

For you, it only takes a few seconds, but for me, it's an invaluable help. Thank you in advance! If there's something you don't like or think could be improved, feel free to email me at m.pabst.en@booksgopublications.com. Your feedback helps me make this book even better!

Welcome to Chapter 2! Here, we'll dive into everything related to your physical, mental, and emotional well-being. You'll learn how to handle mood swings, manage stress and anxiety, and resist social pressure without losing your mind. This chapter is packed with practical advice to help you maintain both physical and mental balance, so you can navigate adolescence with greater confidence and peace of mind. Let's get started!

11. The Gynecologist

One of the most important things you can do for your health as a young woman is to schedule regular visits to a gynecologist. Experts recommend that girls your age make at least one visit per year[3]. A gynecologist is a doctor who specializes in the female reproductive system, and regular visits can help detect infections, ovarian cysts, endometriosis, and other gynecological conditions early on. Your gynecologist can also provide guidance and support regarding issues like menstrual cycle irregularities, sexuality, and birth control options such as the pill. Your first gynecological visit is an opportunity to establish a trusted relationship with a doctor who can support you through the changes of puberty and beyond. During the visit, you'll have the chance to discuss your general health, menstrual cycle, any unusual symptoms, and any questions or concerns you may have. Regular gynecological visits are an essential part of every teenager's health routine. They provide prevention, early diagnosis, education, and support, helping you feel informed and reassured during this important stage of your life.

12. Mood Swings

As a teenager, it's completely normal to experience fluctuating emotions. One day you might feel happy, energetic, or euphoric, and the next, you're suddenly sad, anxious, or unmotivated—often for no apparent reason. Mood swings happen because, as we mentioned earlier, your brain is undergoing major changes, and your hormones are in full swing. While adults experience mood shifts too, teenagers tend to feel them more frequently and more intensely. Here are a few tips to help you manage your mood swings more effectively:

- **Recognize and accept your emotions.** The first step in managing mood swings is understanding that they are normal and a natural part of your development. Accept your emotions without judging yourself.

- **Talk to someone.** Don't bottle up your feelings. Sharing your emotions with a friend, family member, or trusted adult can lighten the emotional load and help you feel better.

---

[3] **Breech, L., Holland-Hall, C., & Hewitt, G. (2005).** *The "well girl" exam.* Journal of Pediatric and Adolescent Gynecology, 18(4), 289-291.

- **Do things you enjoy.** Engaging in activities you love can help balance your emotions. Whether it's playing a sport, learning an instrument, reading, watching movies, painting, or any other hobby, taking time for something you enjoy can boost your mood.

- **Stay active.** Physical activity is a powerful way to reduce stress and improve your mood. This doesn't have to mean intense exercise—even a simple walk can be incredibly beneficial. Exercise releases endorphins, the chemicals that make us feel happy and relaxed.

- **Spend time in nature.** Several studies have shown that being in nature significantly improves mood and mental health[4]. Whenever possible, try to spend some time outdoors.

- **Stay connected with friends and family.** Spending quality time with loved ones can be a great mood booster. However, don't be afraid to take some alone time when needed—solitude can help you reflect and better understand your emotions. Just make sure you don't isolate yourself too much!

13. Stress and Anxiety

Navigating the rollercoaster of puberty can be challenging, especially when stress and anxiety hit you like a tidal wave. Teenage girls are particularly prone to feeling overwhelmed, and there are plenty of reasons for that—body changes, school pressure, friendship conflicts, heartbreak, and even worries about the future. And let's not forget about hormones, which—although invisible—constantly affect your mood and emotions, making everything feel more intense. While adults also experience stress and anxiety, these feelings can be especially powerful during adolescence. Here are some useful tips to help you manage stress and anxiety more effectively:

---

[4] **Pearson, D., & Craig, T. (2014).** *The great outdoors? Exploring the mental health benefits of natural environments.* Frontiers in Psychology, 5.

- **Talk about your worries.** Don't keep everything bottled up. Sharing your concerns with a friend, family member, or trusted adult can ease anxiety and lighten your emotional load.

- **Stay organized.** Good time management can significantly reduce stress. Plan your activities, set priorities, and stick to your schedule as much as possible. Being organized is one of the most underrated secrets for reducing anxiety!

- **Practice relaxation techniques.** Simple techniques like deep breathing, meditation, or yoga can help calm your mind and lower stress levels. Taking a few minutes each day to relax can make a huge difference.

- **Limit caffeine and screen time.** Caffeine can increase anxiety, so try not to overdo it. Also, spending too much time in front of a screen—especially your phone (yes, I know you spend hours scrolling!)—can make stress and anxiety worse. Try to take breaks from digital devices.

- **Get enough sleep.** A good night's rest is essential for managing stress and anxiety. Try to go to bed at the same time every night and make sure you're getting enough hours of sleep. Your brain and body will thank you!

If anxiety or stress ever feels too overwhelming and starts interfering with your daily life, don't hesitate to reach out to a professional. Talking to a therapist or counselor is a sign of strength, not weakness. Asking for help is one of the best things you can do for your mental well-being.

14. Social Pressure

During puberty, social pressure can feel overwhelming. Your friends or classmates might make you feel like you don't belong, whether they mean to or not. You might hear things like, "You're still doing X?" or "You still haven't done Y?"—comments that can make you feel left out or not good enough. Sometimes, social pressure is more subtle and comes from simply comparing yourself to others. Maybe you see your friends excelling in certain areas while you feel stuck. Or maybe you feel pressured to do things you don't actually want to do, just to fit in or avoid being excluded. Giving in to social pressure won't bring real happiness and often leads you away from what's truly best for you. You don't have to do something just because everyone else is doing it. If you ever feel pressured, take a moment to think: Do I really want this, or am I just trying to fit in? Sometimes, all it takes is a little courage to say "no" and choose what's right for you.

Never be afraid to walk away from situations or people that make you uncomfortable. And if the pressure feels too much, talk to someone you trust, like a parent, teacher, or close friend. Remember, being yourself is always the best choice—don't let social pressure define who you are or what you do. Today, social pressure isn't just about fitting in—it's also about appearance. Everywhere you turn—social media, ads, movies, magazines—it seems like all women look perfect. This constant exposure to unrealistic beauty standards can make many girls feel self-conscious, insecure, or unhappy with their bodies. But here's something you need to know: those images don't reflect reality. The pictures you see on social media and in advertisements are often heavily edited to appear flawless[5]. Even celebrities and models who look perfect in photos have insecurities—and they don't look like that in everyday life.

Realizing that what you see in the media is rarely real can help ease the pressure to conform to impossible beauty standards. Instead of chasing an unrealistic ideal, focus on what makes you unique. Learn to appreciate your strengths instead of obsessing over so-called flaws. Taking care of yourself—staying active, eating well, and living a healthy lifestyle—can also boost the way you feel about your body. Most importantly, remember that true beauty comes from within. It's far more important to be healthy and happy than to fit into society's idea of "perfection." Every body is beautiful in its own way, and yours deserves to be appreciated. Learn to love your unique appearance and treat your body with respect and kindness—only then will you overcome social pressure and truly feel confident in your own skin.

---

[5] **Rajanala, S., Maymone, M., & Vashi, N. (2018).** *Selfies-Living in the Era of Filtered Photographs.* JAMA Facial Plastic Surgery, 20(6), 443-444.

15. Self-Esteem and Self-Confidence

Puberty can challenge your self-esteem and confidence, making you question yourself more than ever. But building strong self-confidence starts with recognizing your strengths and qualities—even the small ones. Acknowledge them, be proud of them, and remind yourself that they don't have to be extraordinary to be valuable. It's also important to see mistakes as learning opportunities. Mistakes are a natural part of life, and instead of feeling discouraged by them, try to use them as a springboard for growth. This mindset not only helps improve self-esteem but also makes you more resilient, helping you bounce back from challenges more easily. Another key to boosting confidence is commitment and preparation. Whether you're studying for an exam, working on a project, or stepping into a new challenge, putting in the effort to prepare makes everything feel more manageable. When you work hard to get ready for something, you naturally feel more confident when it's time to face it. Surrounding yourself with positive, supportive people also plays a huge role in building self-esteem. Your family, friends, and mentors can provide encouragement and remind you of your worth, especially in moments of doubt. Choose to spend time with people who lift you up rather than those who bring you down.

Finally, an unexpected but powerful way to boost self-confidence is through fashion and personal style. If you enjoy fashion, taking time to develop your own unique style can make you feel more comfortable in your own skin. Shopping for clothes you love, experimenting with outfits, and following trends that inspire you can help you express your personality and feel more confident. Several studies have shown that people—both men and women—who wear clothes that reflect their personal style tend to have higher self-esteem[6]. When you choose outfits that make you feel good, you're sending a powerful message to the world about who you are. However, remember that confidence doesn't come from expensive clothes or blindly following trends. True self-expression through style is about feeling comfortable and authentic in what you wear, no matter the occasion. At the end of the day, self-esteem isn't about looking perfect—it's

---

[6] **Vingilyte, J., & Khadaroo, A. (2022).** *Personal clothing style and self-concept: Embracing the true, the ideal and the creative self.* Fashion, Style & Popular Culture.

about embracing who you are. The more you appreciate your strengths and express yourself freely, the more confident and self-assured you'll become.

16. Sports

One of the most effective solutions for many of the challenges we've discussed in this chapter—mood swings, stress, anxiety, low self-esteem, and social pressure—is regular physical activity. Sports have an almost magical effect on both the body and mind. When you exercise, your brain releases endorphins—natural chemicals that boost your mood and reduce stress. This makes physical activity an excellent way to ease anxiety and take a break from everyday worries. Beyond its mental health benefits, sports can also help you socially. Team sports, in particular, are a great way to improve social skills, make new friends, and feel a sense of belonging. Working together with teammates toward a common goal can help you build strong, lasting friendships and develop important life skills like teamwork and leadership.

Sports are also essential for your physical health. Regular exercise keeps your heart, lungs, and muscles strong. Experts recommend being active at least three times a week, as it's one of the best things you can do for your overall well-being[7]. It doesn't matter which sport you choose—as long as you find something you enjoy. While team sports can be especially beneficial during adolescence, any kind of movement counts. The most important thing is to stay active, have fun, and keep moving. So, whether it's volleyball, swimming, dance, or even a simple workout at home—get moving! Your body and mind will thank you.

17. Nutrition and Eating Disorders

Let's talk about nutrition. Your body needs a variety of nutrients to function properly: carbohydrates, fats, proteins, vitamins, and minerals. These nutrients provide energy, support tissue repair and growth, and ensure that all your organs work as they should. Understanding the basics of these

---

[7] **Steptoe, A., & Butler, N. (1996).** *Sports participation and emotional wellbeing in adolescents.* The Lancet, 347, 1789-1792.

nutrients will help you see why a healthy, balanced diet is so important. Here's some basic information about them:

- **Carbohydrates.** Carbohydrates are your body's main source of energy. They also help your brain function better by improving concentration and memory, and they serve as your body's primary energy reserve. You'll find them in foods like bread, pasta, and rice. During puberty, your energy needs increase as your body grows rapidly, making carbohydrates essential for fueling your body. Carbohydrates are also found in sweets, but eating too many of them won't provide real benefits.

- **Fats.** Fats provide energy, help your body absorb certain vitamins, and are essential for proper brain function. However, not all fats are the same. Healthy fats, such as those found in nuts, avocados, legumes, and fish, are much better for you than "bad fats" found in fried foods and processed snacks.

- **Protein.** Proteins are like building blocks for your body. They are essential for growth, tissue repair, and muscle development. Protein is found in foods such as meat, fish, eggs, dairy products, and legumes. Including a good source of protein in every meal will help support your body's changes during puberty.

- **Vitamins and minerals.** These are crucial for overall health. Vitamin D and calcium are essential for bone development, vitamin C helps strengthen your immune system, and iron is necessary for transporting oxygen in the blood. A diet rich in fruits, vegetables, and whole grains will help you get the vitamins and minerals your body needs.

Following a balanced diet means eating the right variety of foods in the right proportions to get all the necessary nutrients. No single food contains everything your body needs, so it's important to eat a mix of different foods. A well-balanced diet will provide you with energy, help you focus better in school, support your growth, and strengthen your immune system. Good nutrition will also improve your emotional well-being by helping stabilize your mood and reducing stress. In addition, a healthy diet will help you maintain a healthy weight, reducing the risk of obesity and other related illnesses. Unfortunately, it's not uncommon for teenage girls to struggle with eating disorders such as obesity, bulimia, or anorexia. These conditions can have serious physical and mental health consequences[8], so it's important that you learn more about them:

Obesity

Obesity occurs when the body accumulates too much fat. It can be caused by poor eating habits, lack of physical activity, and/or genetic factors. Being overweight can lead to serious health problems such as diabetes, cardiovascular disease, and joint issues. To prevent obesity, try to eat a balanced diet rich in fruits, vegetables, and proteins. Exercise regularly—not just by playing sports, but also by walking, cycling, or simply playing outside. Avoid junk food and sugary drinks (like industrial fruit juices and soft drinks) as much as possible.

Bulimia

Bulimia is an eating disorder in which people consume large amounts of food in a short period of time ("binges") and then try to eliminate it by making themselves vomit or using laxatives. This behavior is extremely harmful to the body and can cause dehydration, gastrointestinal issues, and severe dental damage. If you find yourself eating compulsively and then trying to get rid of the food, it's crucial to talk to someone you trust immediately. Reach out to a parent, teacher, or doctor—they will know how to support you.

Anorexia

Anorexia is another serious eating disorder where people develop an irrational fear of gaining weight and try to maintain an extremely low body weight by eating very little. This condition can lead to severe health problems such as fatigue, weakness, hair loss, cardiovascular issues, and, in extreme cases, even death. If you notice that you're eating too little or feel overwhelmed by the fear of gaining weight, it's essential to speak with a

---

[8] **Golden, N. H., Katzman, D., Kreipe, R., Stevens, S. L., Sawyer, S., Rees, J., Nicholls, D., & Rome, E. (2003).** *Eating disorders in adolescents: position paper of the Society for Adolescent Medicine.* The Journal of Adolescent Health, 33(6), 496-503.

parent, trusted adult, or doctor as soon as possible. Therapy and medical support are critical for treating anorexia and preventing long-term health consequences.

How to Avoid Eating Disorders

To maintain a healthy relationship with food, aim to eat regularly and in a balanced way, but don't deprive yourself of your favorite foods—just avoid overindulging. Listen to your body: eat when you're hungry and stop when you're full. If you notice that you're developing obsessive thoughts about food or weight, don't hesitate to ask for help. Recognizing the problem and seeking support is the first step toward recovery.

18. Music, Relaxation Techniques, and Mindfulness

Music, relaxation techniques, and mindfulness are powerful tools that can help you manage the stress of puberty. These practices will help you feel calmer, more focused, and in control of your emotions. Here's how they can make a difference in your life.

Music

Music is one of the best remedies for the soul. Whether it's your favorite band, a melody from your instrument, or even singing in the shower, music has the power to lift your mood and reduce stress. Listening to your favorite songs after a long day at school or during tense moments can help you relax and unwind. Try creating a playlist of songs that make you feel good and listen to it whenever you need a break. If you know how to play a musical instrument, using it when you feel anxious or stressed is a great way to clear your mind and let go of worries.

Relaxation Techniques

There are many relaxation techniques you can try, such as deep breathing, progressive muscle relaxation, or meditation. These methods can reduce anxiety, relieve stress, and improve your overall well-being. To start, find a quiet place where you can sit or lie down comfortably. Close your eyes and breathe deeply, focusing on the air moving in and out of your lungs. If you're new to relaxation techniques, you can use an app or an online video to guide you. Simply search for "relaxation techniques" on YouTube or download a meditation app.

Mindfulness

Mindfulness is a practice that helps you "stay anchored in the present moment." It might sound complicated, but it's actually very simple. It means paying close attention to what's happening inside and around you, one moment at a time. Practicing mindfulness can help you manage stress, improve concentration, and increase self-awareness. You can try it in different ways. A simple technique is to sit in a quiet place, close your eyes, and focus on your breathing. If your mind starts to wander (and it will!), gently bring your focus back to your breath. There are also many online resources that can help you practice more advanced mindfulness exercises. Try searching for "mindfulness" on YouTube or downloading a mindfulness app.

19. Sleep

Several studies have shown that teenagers should get between 8 and 10 hours of sleep per night[9]. Getting enough rest makes a huge difference in how you feel, behave, and handle your daily activities. Lack of sleep can have many negative effects. You might feel tired, irritable, and less focused, which can impact your school performance. Sleep deprivation also increases stress and anxiety and can even weaken your immune system, making you more vulnerable to illness. On the other hand, getting enough sleep has many benefits. A good night's rest improves memory, mood, and concentration. It also supports your body's growth and contributes to both physical and mental development. Here are some tips to help you get better sleep:

---

[9] **Paruthi, S., Brooks, L., D'Ambrosio, C., Hall, W., Kotagal, S., Lloyd, R. M., Malow, B., Maski, K., Nichols, C., Quan, S., Rosen, C., Troester, M., & Wise, M. (2016).** *Consensus Statement of the American Academy of Sleep Medicine on the Recommended Amount of Sleep for Healthy Children: Methodology and Discussion.* Journal of Clinical Sleep Medicine: JCSM, 12(11), 1549-1561.

- **Create a sleep routine.** Try to go to bed and wake up at the same time every day. This helps regulate your internal clock and improves the quality of your sleep.

- **Limit screen time before bed.** The blue light emitted by phones, tablets, and computers interferes with melatonin production (the hormone that regulates sleep). Try to turn off screens at least an hour before bedtime.

- **Stay active during the day.** Regular physical activity can help you sleep better. However, avoid intense workouts within two hours before bed, as they can make it harder to fall asleep.

- **Create a comfortable sleep environment.** Keep your bedroom cool, dark, and quiet. If needed, use blackout curtains and earplugs to block out distractions.

- **Avoid caffeine and sugar in the afternoon.** Drinks like coffee, tea, and energy drinks contain caffeine, which keeps you awake. Try to avoid these stimulants later in the day.

- **Relax before bed.** Develop a calming nighttime routine. This could include reading a book, taking a warm bath, or practicing relaxation and mindfulness techniques like the ones we discussed earlier.

20. Ask for Help

Are you struggling with severe and ongoing issues like extreme mood swings, overwhelming stress and anxiety, panic attacks, eating disorders, or serious sleep difficulties? If these challenges become too heavy to bear and start leading to depression, it's essential to seek help. The first step is to confide in someone you trust. Talking to a friend can be a great place to start. You might be surprised at how much your friends understand you and how supportive they can be. Sometimes, simply sharing what you're going through can help ease the emotional burden. Don't forget to talk to your parents as well. They have life experience and may be able to help more than you expect. If speaking to them directly feels difficult, consider writing a letter to express your thoughts—it can be a great way to start the conversation. Other family members, like aunts, uncles, or grandparents, can also offer valuable support if you have a strong relationship with them. If talking to friends and family isn't enough, consider seeking professional help. Psychologists, psychiatrists, and therapists are trained to help people manage depression, chronic anxiety, eating disorders, and other serious emotional struggles. There is no shame in asking for help. In fact, recognizing that you need support and seeking it out is a sign of strength and maturity. No one should have to face difficult times alone—help is available, and you deserve to feel better.

Chapter 3: 10 Mysteries of Sexuality

Now we've reached Chapter 3, where we're going to dive into one of the most intriguing topics—one I'm sure you've been curious about: sexuality. We'll be talking about sex—a word you might be familiar with, but one that probably still raises a lot of questions for you. And let's be honest, I know you and your friends are already talking about this! In this chapter, we'll clear up some of the biggest myths about sex and give you real, honest answers to the questions you might be too shy to ask. So, get ready to learn everything you've ever wanted to know about sex—but were afraid to ask.

21. The Male Reproductive System

Now that you've learned about your own reproductive system, it's a good idea to understand the male reproductive system as well. After all, sex is a shared experience! But even beyond that, this is important knowledge for you to have. The male reproductive system consists of the penis, testicles, scrotum, epididymis, vas deferens, seminal vesicles, prostate, and bulbourethral glands. Here's what you need to know:

- **The penis.** The penis is the external organ used for both urination and ejaculation (which we'll discuss later). It is made up of erectile tissue, which fills with blood during sexual arousal, allowing for an erection when a man experiences sexual excitement.

- **The testicles.** These are two glands inside the scrotum (the protective skin that surrounds them). Their main job is to produce sperm and testosterone—the primary male sex hormone.

- **The scrotum.** This is the sack of skin that holds the testicles. Its main function is to regulate temperature for sperm production by contracting and relaxing, moving the testicles closer to or farther from the body depending on the temperature.

- **The epididymis.** This is a structure above the testicles where sperm mature and are stored before ejaculation.

- **The vas deferens.** These are the tubes that transport sperm from the testicles to the seminal vesicles. They play a crucial role in the process of ejaculation.

- **The seminal vesicles.** These produce a fluid that nourishes sperm, making up a large portion of semen, which is essential for fertility.

- **The prostate.** This gland, located beneath the bladder, produces a fluid that helps sperm stay mobile and survive inside the vagina.

- **The bulbourethral glands.** Also known as Cowper's glands, these produce a pre-ejaculatory fluid that lubricates the urethra and neutralizes acidity, creating a safer environment for sperm.

22. Sexual Arousal

It's completely normal for girls and boys your age to start experiencing sexual arousal—the body's natural physical and psychological response to erotic stimuli. But what exactly does it mean to be sexually aroused? When a woman is aroused, her vagina produces natural lubrication mainly from the vaginal walls, with additional secretions from the Bartholin's glands. These fluids lubricate the vagina, making intercourse less painful and more pleasurable. In addition, the clitoris, which is the most sensitive part of the vulva, swells and becomes more reactive during arousal. The clitoris has thousands of nerve endings, making it highly sensitive to touch and stimulation. Sexual arousal can happen at any time, sometimes even for no clear reason. However, it is usually triggered by sexual stimuli, such as erotic thoughts, images, videos, or physical contact with someone you're attracted to (such as foreplay, which we'll discuss soon). When a woman feels aroused and her vagina becomes moist, it means her body is preparing for possible intercourse, making penetration easier and the experience more comfortable and enjoyable. Of course, sexual arousal isn't just for girls. Boys experience arousal through erection, which happens when the penis becomes rigid and erect due to increased blood flow into the erectile tissues. While the physical signs of arousal are different for boys and girls, the biological process is similar, relying on a complex interaction of hormones and nervous system responses. Sexual arousal is a natural and normal part of human sexuality. It's not something to feel ashamed or embarrassed about—it's simply part of how the human body works.

23. What Is Sex and How Does It Happen?

Do you already know what sex is like? It's a deeply personal experience that can bring out different emotions for everyone. From a technical standpoint, sexual intercourse happens when your partner's penis is inserted into your vagina. As your two bodies come together, pleasure increases for both of you. During intercourse, the clitoris, vaginal lips, and vagina swell and become more sensitive, enhancing sensation. Intercourse can lead to orgasm. For men, orgasm is connected to ejaculation, which occurs when seminal fluid containing sperm is expelled from the penis. Male ejaculation typically marks the end of intercourse, as the penis returns to its normal, soft state. Women, of course, can also orgasm during intercourse, and sometimes even experience multiple orgasms. A female orgasm is usually accompanied by intense, pleasurable muscle contractions that last a few seconds. The brain also plays a major role in female orgasm, releasing hormones like oxytocin and dopamine, which create feelings of euphoria and well-being. However, women don't always reach orgasm during intercourse—and that's completely normal. If you find that you don't achieve orgasm often, remember that communication with your partner is key. Talking openly about what feels good can help make future experiences more enjoyable and increase your chances of reaching orgasm. Keep in mind that everyone is different, and sexual pleasure is a highly individual experience. What works for one person may not work for another. And most importantly—if your partner ejaculates inside your vagina, pregnancy is possible. To prevent this, it's essential to use contraception like condoms or birth control pills, which we'll discuss in one of the next sections.

24. Having Sex for the First Time

Your first time can be exciting, but it's also normal to feel a little nervous or unsure. That's why it's important to have sex only when you feel truly ready and with someone you trust. Before you take this step, talk openly with your partner about your feelings, concerns, and expectations. Remember, sex should always be based on respect, communication, and mutual consent. Take things slowly and gently, making sure that both of you feel comfortable. For most young women, first-time intercourse can result in the hymen tearing. The hymen is a thin membrane that partially covers the vaginal opening. Its rupture may cause slight bleeding, which is completely normal during first intercourse. So if you notice a little blood, don't worry—it's part of the process! Here are some useful tips for your first time:

- **Communicate.** Tell your partner what you like and what makes you uncomfortable. Ask them how they feel, too. Open communication is the key to a positive sexual experience for both of you.

- **Use a condom.** Always use a condom to prevent sexually transmitted infections (STIs) and unintended pregnancy. We'll discuss condom use in more detail later.

- **Take your time.** There's no rush. Explore at your own pace and enjoy the moment with your partner.

- **Relax.** It's completely normal to feel nervous the first time, but try to breathe and stay calm. Don't put pressure on yourself—nobody is perfect at sex right away.

25. Masturbation

Masturbation involves stimulating the sexual organs, usually with the hands, to experience pleasure. For girls, this includes stimulation of the clitoris, vaginal lips, and other sensitive areas of the vulva. Masturbation often leads to orgasm and can be a natural way to explore your body. Masturbation can be stimulated by imagination, where you think about or picture situations that have aroused you—or that you believe would arouse you. It can also be triggered by watching sexually stimulating images or videos. However, most sexologists agree that the "healthiest" form of masturbation is guided by imagination, rather than relying on pornographic videos or images[10]. Using your imagination allows for a more personal connection with your own desires and fantasies, without depending on external influences, which can be exaggerated and don't always reflect real-life sexuality. It may seem surprising, but masturbation has several benefits. It can help relieve stress and anxiety, improve your mood, and even promote better sleep. It's also a way to learn more about your body and what you enjoy sexually. Experts in sexual health consider masturbation to be a normal part of human sexuality. That said, while masturbation is natural and has its benefits, it's important not to overdo it. Masturbating too frequently can disrupt sleep, interfere with concentration at school or daily activities, and even affect relationships with friends, family, or a partner. If you ever feel that masturbation is becoming too much of a distraction, try engaging in other enjoyable activities that help you relax, like playing sports, reading a book, or spending time with friends. Masturbation is a natural way to explore your body and understand your desires, but like anything else, it's important to practice it in moderation and with awareness, without overindulging.

26. Foreplay

Foreplay is a great way to explore sexuality without going all the way to full sexual intercourse. It includes a mix of kissing, cuddling, caressing, massaging, genital touching, and body-to-body contact—all of which can provide a lot of pleasure without penetration. Foreplay is important because it helps both partners become aroused. For girls, stimulation through touch and caressing increases natural vaginal lubrication, which makes sex more comfortable and reduces the risk of pain. For boys, it helps maintain a firm erection and mentally prepare for intercourse. Foreplay is also a great way to learn more about your own body and what feels good. In a way, it's like warming up before a workout! Even though foreplay doesn't involve penetration, there is still a risk of unintended pregnancy if genital fluids come into contact with your private areas. To avoid these risks, make sure your partner's semen never comes into direct contact with your

---

[10] **Zimmer, F., & Imhoff, R. (2020).** *Abstinence from Masturbation and Hypersexuality.* Archives of Sexual Behavior, 49, 1333-1343.

vulva—even small amounts can pose a risk. To fully enjoy foreplay without anxiety, talk openly with your partner. Set clear boundaries together and make sure they respect your comfort levels. If you ever feel uncomfortable, don't be afraid to speak up and stop.

27. Preventing STIs and Unintended Pregnancy

Condoms are the most effective way to prevent sexually transmitted infections (STIs) and unintended pregnancy. They are easy to use and highly reliable when used correctly. A condom forms a physical barrier that prevents sperm from entering the vagina, reducing the risk of pregnancy. It also protects against viruses and bacteria that can cause infections. Using a condom during sex is crucial for both your health and your partner's. Your partner should know how to properly use a condom. If he is unsure, here are a few important best practices to keep in mind before having sex:

- **Check the expiration date.** Always check the expiration date on the package to make sure the condom is still effective and safe to use.

- **Open it carefully.** Tear open the package gently to avoid damaging the condom. Most condom wrappers have a notched edge to indicate where to open them.

- **Make sure the erection is firm.** A condom should only be put on when the penis is fully erect.

- **Unroll it to the base of the penis.** Pinch the tip of the condom with two fingers to remove excess air, place it over the tip of the penis, and unroll it all the way down to the base. This prevents air bubbles, which can cause breakage.

- **Dispose of it properly after use.** After sex, remove the condom carefully, tie it in a knot to prevent leakage, and throw it in the trash—never in the toilet.

- **Store condoms correctly.** Keep them in a cool, dry place. Avoid storing them in hot or humid environments, as this can weaken the material.

Another commonly used method of contraception is the pill. The birth control pill is an oral medication that contains synthetic hormones, primarily estrogen and progesterone, which prevent ovulation. Without ovulation, there's no egg available for fertilization, so pregnancy cannot occur. However, the pill does not protect against STIs and should never be used as a replacement for condoms, especially when having sex with someone who is not your long-term partner. Before starting the pill, it's essential to consult a gynecologist. This is necessary to determine which formula best suits your needs and to discuss any potential side effects or risks. The pill can sometimes cause mild side effects, such as nausea, headaches, weight fluctuations, or mood swings. However, many women experience no major side effects, and in some cases, the benefits outweigh the risks. In addition to preventing pregnancy, the pill may also offer other advantages, such as reducing acne, regulating menstrual cycles, and easing particularly painful premenstrual symptoms. Despite its benefits, it's crucial to follow your doctor's instructions carefully to ensure its effectiveness and minimize any potential risks.

28. The Right Age to Have Sex and Sexual Abuse

There is no "perfect" age to start having sex. Everyone moves at their own pace, and it's important to wait until you feel physically and emotionally ready. But if I can give you a personal piece of advice, don't rush into it—there's absolutely no need to hurry. Some people feel ready earlier, while others feel ready later, and that's completely normal. The key is to listen to yourself and not let outside pressure influence your decision. Sex should always be a personal choice, and you should never feel like you have to do it just because others are. Of course, consent is essential in any sexual relationship, at any age. Both partners must fully agree and feel comfortable with what they're doing. If one of you isn't ready, that feeling must be respected, and it's important to wait until the time is right. It's critical to understand the seriousness of sexual abuse, especially when it involves teenagers like you. Sexual abuse is a crime that involves any non-consensual sexual act. These acts are not only illegal, but they also cause severe emotional and psychological harm to the victims. Sexual abuse doesn't just mean forced intercourse—it can also include unwanted touching, coercion, sexual harassment, or manipulation. Abuse can be committed by adults or other teenagers, and sometimes, unfortunately, even by people you know—such as friends, family members, or teachers. If you or someone you know has been sexually abused, it's crucial to speak up immediately. Tell a trusted adult, such as a parent, teacher, or school counselor. You can also reach out to authorities like the police or child protection services. Many communities have organizations dedicated to helping and supporting victims of sexual abuse. Reporting abuse is not just about protecting yourself—it's also about protecting others who could be at risk. Although talking about sexual abuse can feel scary or embarrassing, always remember: it is never your fault. Seeking help is the bravest and best thing you can do.

29. Pornography

Pornography is a sensitive but important topic to discuss. Today, it is easily accessible, and many teenagers come across it or actively seek it out. However, the most important thing to understand is that porn does not represent reality when it comes to sex. In fact, pornography almost always depicts exaggerated and unrealistic situations that do not reflect real-life sexuality. The scenes in pornography are staged, carefully filmed, and edited to be entertaining—not educational. That's why it's essential not to base your expectations about sex on what you see in porn, because real experiences are very different. Pornography can also negatively influence your perception of sex. Although it is more commonly consumed—and sometimes overused—by men, it's important to be aware of its potential effects on anyone, including you. If watched excessively, porn can become addictive, altering how you think about intimacy and relationships. Porn can serve as a way to explore sexuality, but it must be approached responsibly. The key is to not let it distort your understanding of real-life sex, relationships, and intimacy.

30. The Most Common Myths About Sex

Many sexual myths circulate among girls your age (I guessed right, didn't I?), and they can be confusing. Let's clear up some of the most common misconceptions about sex.

- **Myth:** A woman can only feel pleasure through penetration.

- **Reality:** Female sexual pleasure doesn't come exclusively from penetration. In fact, for many women, clitoral stimulation is the key to orgasm. That's why communication with your partner is essential—so they understand how to please you and ensure a satisfying sexual experience.

- **Myth:** You can't get pregnant without penetration.
- **Reality:** Pregnancy is possible even without penetration if semen (even small amounts) comes into direct contact with the vaginal area.

- **Myth:** Condoms reduce pleasure during sex.
- **Reality:** Condoms are designed to be extremely thin and should not significantly reduce pleasure for either partner. Many high-quality options are available that minimize discomfort during sex. In most cases, the difference in sensation is minimal and largely psychological.

- **Myth:** Everyone has sex during their teenage years.
- **Reality:** Not everyone has sex in their teens—and that's completely okay. Everyone moves at their own pace, and there's no rush. If you haven't had sex yet, you're not late or behind anyone.

- **Myth:** Girls don't enjoy sex as much as boys.
- **Reality:** Of course girls experience pleasure during sex—and their pleasure is just as important as a man's.

- **Myth:** Sex is always painful for women.
- **Reality:** Sex should not be painful. If it is, you may need more foreplay to allow for proper lubrication, or you can use lubricants to make it more comfortable.

- **Myth:** Men always have to take the initiative in sex.
- **Reality:** Both partners can take the lead. Open communication about desires and boundaries is what makes sex a healthy and enjoyable experience for both people.

Chapter 4: 10 Mysteries About Boys, Love, and Relationships

Welcome to Chapter 4, where we explore the fascinating and sometimes confusing world of boys, love, and relationships. Are you ready to understand the male universe a little better and build healthy, meaningful connections? Perfect! Here, you'll find answers to many of your biggest questions. Let's start with one of the most important ones.

31. The Difference Between Attraction and Love

One of the biggest questions at your age is: what's the difference between attraction and love? Attraction is that instant spark you feel when you see someone who makes your heart race. It's an almost instinctive reaction—you're drawn to a person's appearance, their scent, or the way they carry themselves. Physical attraction and immediate chemistry play a major role. You might see a good-looking guy and—BAM!—you're instantly captivated. But here's the thing: attraction is often shallow. You don't need to know someone deeply to feel drawn to them. It's like having a crush on a celebrity—he looks amazing, but you don't actually know him!

Love, on the other hand, is a completely different story. Think of it like your favorite dish—one where you know every ingredient and love it, even if it's not the most beautiful plate on the table. Love goes far beyond physical attraction. It happens when you truly get to know someone—their strengths, weaknesses, quirks—and still cherish them, flaws and all. It's a deep emotional connection built over time, based on trust, respect, and genuine affection. Finding love isn't easy, and it takes effort from both partners. But just like mastering your favorite recipe, it's absolutely worth it!

32. How to Attract the Right Kind of Boy

Do you have a crush on a guy but don't know how to catch his attention? Are you convinced he's the right one for you but unsure how to make him notice you? Attracting a good guy—the kind who is respectful, kind, and capable of building a healthy relationship—starts with one essential rule: be yourself. Authenticity and sincerity are some of the most attractive qualities you can have. Pretending to be someone you're not just to impress someone is not only exhausting but also unsustainable. A relationship built on pretense will collapse just as quickly as it started. A good man is drawn to someone who is genuine and confident in who they are—so don't be afraid to show your true interests, passions, and personality. Self-esteem and confidence naturally make you more attractive. Take care of yourself—not just physically, but mentally as well. Stay active, pursue your passions, and keep learning new things. Confidence isn't just about looking good; it's about having goals, dreams, and the determination to achieve them. That kind of mindset is magnetic and will naturally attract someone who values independence and ambition. Respect and kindness matter.

A guy appreciates being treated with consideration, just as you do. That doesn't mean you have to agree with everything he says, but it does mean treating him the way you'd like to be treated. Listening, showing respect for his opinions, and being kind are all signs that you genuinely care. A positive attitude is also incredibly attractive. Try to see the good in situations and face challenges with resilience. Positivity is contagious, and someone who approaches life with enthusiasm and a strong mindset naturally draws others in. It won't just make your life better—it will also attract a partner who values optimism and strength. Lastly, show interest in the people and things that matter to him. Taking the time to understand his world—whether it's his family, close friends, or passions—demonstrates that you care beyond just the romantic aspect. It shows that you're ready to build something meaningful together.

33. Femininity

Femininity is a concept that encompasses a range of qualities traditionally associated with women. However, being feminine doesn't mean being weak or submissive—it's about embracing the traits that make you feel confident, comfortable, and authentic. In modern society, women can excel in any field, take on leadership roles, and achieve anything men can. But femininity remains a valuable and positive trait, no matter what career path or lifestyle you choose.

Femininity includes elements such as grace, kindness, sensitivity, and self-care. It's not about fitting into outdated stereotypes but rather finding a personal balance that allows you to feel empowered in your own skin. Expressing femininity can boost self-esteem by helping you embrace and celebrate your unique qualities as a woman. Many men find confidence in femininity attractive—not because of outdated gender roles, but because self-assurance in who you are is inherently appealing. Here are some ways to express your femininity in a way that feels natural and authentic to you:

- **Take care of your appearance.** Looking after yourself is one of the simplest ways to express femininity. This doesn't mean heavy makeup or wearing a specific type of clothing—it's about choosing outfits that make you feel good, maintaining healthy hair and skin, and practicing good hygiene.

- **Be kind and gracious.** Qualities like kindness, empathy, and good manners are often associated with femininity. Being a good listener and treating others with warmth and respect will not only enhance your relationships but also reinforce your confidence in your own character.

- **Be authentic.** True femininity isn't about fitting into a mold—it's about embracing what feels right for you. Whether you prefer a classic, elegant style or a more casual and modern approach, confidence in your choices is what makes femininity shine.

- **Express your emotions.** Don't be afraid to show what you feel. Understanding and expressing your emotions in a healthy way—whether joy, sadness, or excitement—demonstrates emotional intelligence and self-awareness, which are both attractive and empowering qualities.

- **Invest in personal growth.** Femininity isn't just about appearance—it's also about developing your mind and spirit. Pursuing education, exploring your passions, and setting meaningful goals all contribute to a well-rounded and confident version of yourself. Dedication and ambition are powerful aspects of modern femininity.

34. Romance

Let's talk about romance. It might sound old-fashioned, but trust me—romance is alive and well. In love, romance is essential because it adds magic, depth, and emotional connection to a relationship. Being romantic means showing your partner that your heart beats only for them, expressing your feelings in a sincere way, without any ulterior motives. Romance can be found in the little things—small gestures, affectionate words, gentle touches, patience, and unwavering support. It's about making your partner feel cherished and special. Organizing outings or shared activities is a great way to express romance. A picnic in the park, a walk in a meaningful place, or an evening spent enjoying a common hobby can strengthen your bond and create unforgettable memories. Romance doesn't have to be extravagant or expensive; in fact, the simplest and most heartfelt gestures often mean the most.

Sincere compliments are another powerful way to express romance. Let your partner know what you admire about them—whether it's their smile, their kindness, or their support. Avoid exaggerated clichés; authenticity is key. When compliments come from the heart, they make your partner feel genuinely appreciated and loved. Equally important is recognizing romance in your boyfriend's actions. A romantic partner might surprise you with little gestures, like bringing you flowers, writing sweet messages, or planning thoughtful surprises. Appreciate these moments and reciprocate them in your own way. Mutual romance strengthens a relationship and deepens emotional intimacy. Being romantic isn't difficult or embarrassing—it's simply a way of showing your partner that they hold a special place in your life. Creating an atmosphere of love and appreciation through romance leads to a stronger, happier relationship. So don't hold back—express your feelings, make small gestures of love, and embrace romance. It's an essential ingredient in any lasting and fulfilling relationship.

35. The First Date

The first date can feel nerve-wracking, but don't stress—I'm here to help! First of all, does the guy always have to be the one to ask the girl out? According to old-fashioned rules of chivalry, maybe. But times have changed! If you like someone, there's nothing wrong with making the first move. Asking a guy out is just about getting to know each other—so why not? Once you've both agreed to go out, it's time to decide where. A cozy café, an ice cream shop, or a walk in the park are great choices. Avoid loud, crowded places where you'll struggle to hear each other. Since the whole point of a first date is to talk and connect, a noisy environment is the worst setting.

During the date, listen attentively to what he says. Show genuine interest in his words, dreams, and passions—it's one of the easiest ways to build a connection. And please, put your phone on silent (or better yet, away). Nothing kills the mood like constant notifications interrupting your conversation. Most importantly, be yourself. Don't try to impress him with exaggerated stories or by acting like someone you're not. True confidence comes from being comfortable with who you are, strengths and weaknesses included. Speak openly about yourself—you might discover you have more in common than you thought. Finally, know that it's perfectly normal to feel a little nervous. He probably is too! Just try to relax and enjoy the moment. And if there's any awkwardness, a lighthearted joke can work wonders to break the ice.

36. Kissing, Foreplay, and Making Love

So, your date with the guy you like is going well, and you feel like things might lead to a kiss... or maybe more? That's exciting! But how can you make sure the moment feels natural and special? Let's explore it together.

Kissing

A kiss is one of the most intimate and meaningful gestures you can share with someone. If the moment feels right, lean in slowly, look into his eyes, and let it happen naturally. Don't overthink technique—a spontaneous, genuine kiss is far better than a calculated, "perfect" one. The key is to be present in the moment and let your emotions guide you.

Foreplay

We've already talked about how important foreplay is before sexual intimacy. Just like athletes warm up before a game, foreplay helps both partners feel comfortable, aroused, and connected before intercourse. It plays a crucial role for women, as it encourages natural vaginal lubrication, reducing discomfort or pain during sex. But it's just as important for men—it helps them become more aroused and maintain a strong erection. Beyond the physical benefits, foreplay allows partners to explore each other's bodies and understand what brings them pleasure. Communication is key here—being open about what you like, what feels good, and setting clear boundaries creates an experience that is enjoyable and respectful for both partners.

Making Love

Making love is different from just having sex. It's not just a physical act—it's a deep, intimate experience with someone you truly connect with. While sex without emotional involvement can feel impersonal and focused solely on physical pleasure, making love is about affection, trust, and mutual care. Every touch and every gesture should reflect the love and connection you share. And one final, important note: real intimacy is nothing like what you see in pornography. Those scenes are scripted and staged, and they don't reflect real emotions, genuine connection, or true pleasure. In reality, intimacy is much more beautiful because it's personal, authentic, and built on mutual trust.

37. Consent, Respect, and Intimacy

Let's talk about three essential pillars of any loving relationship: consent, respect, and intimacy. These elements are the foundation of a healthy, fulfilling relationship. Ready? Let's dive in.

Consent

Consent is absolutely non-negotiable in any intimate interaction, whether it's a kiss or something more. It means that both people must be fully and enthusiastically on board with what's happening. A hesitant "maybe" isn't enough—you need a clear, confident "yes." If you're unsure about taking the next step, say so clearly. Your feelings matter, and you should never feel pressured into anything you're not ready for. Remember: "no" means no, and silence is never a substitute for consent. If necessary, state your boundaries firmly. And don't be afraid to change your mind—consent isn't permanent. You can withdraw it at any time, and your partner must respect that immediately.

Respect

Respect is the foundation of every strong relationship. It means truly listening to your partner's thoughts, feelings, and concerns with empathy. It means never pressuring them into something they're uncomfortable with. Respect also means avoiding hurtful comments, demeaning jokes, or dismissing your partner's emotions. Healthy relationships are built on mutual understanding and trust, where both people feel valued and safe.

Intimacy

Intimacy is about much more than physical connection. It's the deep emotional bond that develops over time between two people. While sex can be one part of intimacy, true intimacy is also found in the small moments—a shared laugh, a heartfelt conversation, a warm embrace, or simply enjoying each other's presence in silence. There's no rush to reach deep intimacy—it grows naturally with time, trust, and patience. The best relationships are built step by step, at a pace that feels right for both partners.

38. Heartbreak

Alright, dear teenager, let's talk about one of life's toughest—but completely inevitable—experiences: heartbreak. I know, it can feel like the end of the world, but trust me, it's not. Almost everyone goes through it at some point, and it's simply part of the journey toward finding true love. Think about it—even celebrities, movie superheroes, and the people you admire have had their hearts broken at least once. It's a universal experience, so don't think you're unlucky just because your first love didn't turn out as you'd hoped. The hard truth? Most first loves aren't meant to last.

When you're dealing with heartbreak, the first and most important thing to do is talk about it. Open up to a friend, a family member, or someone who can help you process your emotions. Bottling up your feelings will only make the pain last longer. As tempting as it might be to isolate yourself, try not to. Surround yourself with people who make you feel good—even if, at first, you don't feel like being around anyone. Healing takes time, so don't rush the process. Do things that bring you joy: watch your favorite movies, listen to music, or dive into a hobby you love. The goal isn't to erase your emotions, but to remind yourself that there's still happiness to be found, even after heartbreak. And yes, sometimes a little chocolate really can help. Most importantly, remember that this pain is temporary. The sadness you feel today won't last forever. In time, your heart will heal, and you'll be ready for a new love story. And who knows? Maybe your next relationship will be the one that truly lasts. Keep your head up and never stop believing in love.

39. What It Means to Be a Couple

You've found the guy of your dreams, and now you're officially together—congratulations! But what does it really mean to be in a relationship? It's not just about posting cute pictures on Instagram. It's so much more than that. Being in a committed relationship means sharing an important part of your life with another person. There are plenty of wonderful moments—affection, mutual support, and feeling like the star of your own romantic movie. But relationships also come with responsibilities and challenges that shouldn't be overlooked. First and foremost, being present matters. It's not enough to just send an occasional text. Being in a relationship means truly listening to your partner, standing by them in tough times, and celebrating life's happy moments together.

Compromise is key. You won't always get your way, and sometimes, you'll have to do things just because they matter to your partner. Maybe that means watching an action movie at the cinema instead of your usual romantic one. But look at it this way—learning to compromise is a life skill that will serve you well in every relationship, not just romantic ones. Respect and trust are the foundation of a strong relationship. Without them, things will eventually fall apart. Respect his personal space, his friends, and his interests, even if they don't always align with yours. And just as importantly, trust him and be worthy of his trust. Excessive jealousy can quickly destroy a relationship, so if you want things to last, focus on building security and confidence in each other. It's also important to maintain a balance between your personal life and your relationship. Don't lose yourself in being "his girlfriend." Keep nurturing your own passions, friendships, and ambitions. A healthy relationship is one where both partners grow together and as individuals. And finally—have fun! Laugh together, create unforgettable memories, and don't take things too seriously. Relationships have their ups and downs, but with love, effort, and mutual understanding, you can overcome any obstacle together.

40. Communication in a Relationship

Finally, let's talk about one of the most crucial aspects of any relationship: communication. Clear, honest communication is the key to understanding each other, avoiding unnecessary conflicts, and building a strong emotional connection. If something is bothering you, don't bottle it up—address it as soon as possible. If your partner does something you don't like or if you feel neglected, bring it up calmly and openly. The longer you wait, the bigger the issue can become. Being upfront about your feelings, preferences, and boundaries helps prevent unnecessary arguments and misunderstandings.

But communication isn't just about problems—it's also about sharing your emotions. If you're happy, say it. If you're feeling down, stressed, or overwhelmed, let your partner know. You don't have to be Wonder Woman and suffer in silence. Opening up can feel vulnerable, but it's how you create a real and meaningful connection. And remember, communication is a two-way street. Just as you want to be heard, your partner does too. When he shares his worries, joys, or thoughts, listen actively. Show genuine interest, make eye contact, and respond thoughtfully. Sometimes, the best thing you can do is simply be there—a silent hug can often say more than words. Finally, don't forget to keep a sense of humor. Not every conversation has to be serious. Laughter can ease tension, strengthen your bond, and remind you both to enjoy the journey together.

Chapter 5: 10 Mysteries About Social Life and Friendships

Friendships are a fundamental part of life, especially during adolescence. Friends provide support, fun, and personal growth. But what does it really mean to be a good friend? How do you build and maintain strong friendships? Let's dive in!

41. What Is a Friend?

What is a friend? No, I'm not talking about someone who just adds you on Instagram or sends you funny memes (although that's always nice). A real friend is so much more than that. A true friend is someone who's there for you—both in good times and bad. It's someone you can share your successes and failures with, knowing they'll always have your back. Whether you're having the best day ever or going through something tough, a true friend will be there to listen. A real friend accepts you exactly as you are, with all your strengths and flaws. You don't have to pretend to be someone else or act a certain way just to impress them. With a true friend, you can be yourself—no mask, no filter. Even if you embarrass yourself sometimes, a real friend won't judge you—they'll laugh with you, not at you.

A good friend is also loyal. They won't betray you or talk behind your back. If you have a problem, you know you can count on them. A true friend wants the best for you—they won't just tell you what you want to hear, but will give you honest advice, even when it's hard to swallow. In short, a friend is someone who makes your life better just by being in it. They're your companion, your confidant, and your ally. So if you have true friends, hold on to them. And if you haven't found them yet, don't worry—real friendships take time to grow. Finally, don't forget that in today's society, it's perfectly normal for girls to have both male and female friends—no discrimination!

42. How to Make Friends

Making friends is one of the most important and rewarding things you can do, especially as a teenager. But how do you actually make new friends? There's no magic button for friendship—it takes effort, but it's worth it. First, you need to have an active life. You won't make friends if you spend all your time playing video games alone or glued to your phone every time you leave the house. Get involved in offline activities that interest you—join a club, play a sport, or start a hobby. This will not only help you meet people who share your interests, but also make starting conversations easier.

Most importantly, be yourself. Don't try to change who you are just to fit in. True friendships are built on authenticity. People appreciate honesty and sincerity, so don't be afraid to show your true personality, even if you think you're a little weird. (Spoiler: we're all a little weird!). Here are some additional tips for making new friends:

- **Be proactive.** Don't wait for others to approach you—start the conversation. Even a simple "Hey, how's it going?" could lead to a great friendship.

- **Listen attentively.** Show genuine interest in what people are saying. Good listening skills are one of the most valuable traits in friendships.

- **Give sincere compliments.** A simple, honest compliment can break the ice and create a positive vibe—as long as it's genuine. No exaggerated praise like "You're the best volleyball player ever!"

- **Be trustworthy.** Keep your promises and be someone people can count on. Trust is the foundation of any strong friendship.

- **Create shared experiences.** Do things together: going on a trip, playing sports, or even just studying together. Shared moments create lasting bonds.

43. How to Keep Your Friends

You've made a new friend, and that's great! But now comes the hardest part—keeping that friendship strong. Friendships, like any other relationship, need care and attention to last. That means you have to make an effort to stay in touch. You don't need to see each other every day, but a quick text or call now and then can make a big difference. Show your friend that you care and that you're thinking about them, even when life gets busy. And just like in romantic relationships, if something is bothering you, speak up. Addressing small issues right away can prevent them from turning into bigger misunderstandings later on.

Another key to keeping a friendship strong is mutual support. Be there for your friend when things get tough, not just when everything's great. If they need to talk or have a problem, listen and offer support. You don't need to have all the answers—sometimes, just being there is enough. Showing empathy and understanding will only make your bond stronger. And finally, don't forget to have fun together. Friendships should be full of joy and laughter. Plan fun activities, share inside jokes, and never take yourselves too seriously. A good friendship is one that makes life better—so don't let it fade away.

44. Don't Be a Follower

Let's talk about something that's definitely not cool—copying what your friends do, especially when it's reckless or dangerous. I get it, you want to fit in and not feel left out. But trust me, risking your health or reputation just to follow the crowd isn't worth it. Take, for example, those stupid dares that some people do just to show off—climbing over train tracks, running across a busy road at the last second, playing with firecrackers, or shoplifting just for fun. Doing something just because your friends are doing it doesn't make you brave—it makes you stupid. Your safety comes first, and a real friend would never pressure you into doing something dangerous. The same goes for drinking, smoking, or even drugs. Just because your friends do it doesn't mean you have to. There's a whole chapter on addictions later in this book, and you'll see just how harmful these habits can be. There's nothing cool about damaging your health just to fit in.

Think for yourself—don't let others push you into things you don't want to do.

Another classic example? Tattoos. Just because your friends are getting them doesn't mean you should rush into it. Tattoos are permanent, and removing them is painful and expensive. Wait until you're older and completely sure about what you want. A spur-of-the-moment tattoo could be a lifetime regret. At the end of the day, copying others—especially when it's reckless or questionable—doesn't make you cool. In fact, it shows a lack of confidence in your own decisions. Be independent, think for yourself, and choose what's truly right for you.

45. Toxic Friends

Now let's talk about a serious and difficult topic: toxic friends. These are the people who drag you down instead of lifting you up. And we're not just talking about friends who treat you badly—but also those who push you into reckless, harmful, or straight-up wrong behavior. Imagine having a friend who encourages you to smoke, bully someone, steal, or take drugs. When you're around them, you might feel pressured to go along with it so you don't seem "weak" or "boring". But this kind of pressure can lead you to make bad choices, risk your safety, and even turn into someone you don't want to be. So how do you know if you're stuck with toxic friends? Pay attention to how you feel when you're around them. If you often feel stressed, anxious, or pressured to do things that don't sit right with you, that's a red flag. Friends should make you feel good—not like you're constantly walking on eggshells.

What can you do? You have two choices. First, you can cut ties completely. I know this isn't easy, but sometimes putting yourself first is necessary. If a toxic friend doesn't respect your boundaries and keeps dragging you into situations you're uncomfortable with, walking away may be the best decision. Second, if you think the friendship can be saved, you can try to maintain it without following their bad habits. Lead by example—show them that you can have fun without taking risks. Maybe, over time, they'll follow your lead and change for the better. No matter what, don't forget that you deserve better. You deserve friends who respect and support you. Never sacrifice your safety, integrity, or happiness just to hold on to a friendship. Be strong, make the right choices, and surround yourself with people who bring out the best in you.

46. Being Part of a Group

Being part of a group is great. Whether it's a volleyball team, a chess club, or a group of friends who love shopping, groups give you a sense of belonging and allow you to pursue your passions with people who share your interests. Having something in common is a powerful way to build strong friendships. Imagine you're on a volleyball team. Sharing victories and defeats, training together, and improving as a group creates a bond that goes beyond just having fun. The same goes for any hobby or interest—finding people who share your passions can greatly enrich your social life.

However, belonging to a group should never be an excuse to exclude or discriminate against others. Unfortunately, some groups become too closed off and start seeing outsiders as "different" or "inferior." That's never a good thing. Don't turn your group into an exclusive club where others aren't welcome. Instead, use your position to be inclusive and invite new people in. Not only will this make the group stronger and more diverse, but it will also help you make new friends. Being kind and open to others is a valuable quality—one that will make you even more respected within your group.

47. Empathy

Empathy is the ability to put yourself in someone else's shoes—to understand how they feel and respond with kindness and compassion. It's one of the most important skills for making friends and building strong, healthy relationships. Imagine your friend had a terrible day at school. Instead of brushing it off, try to imagine how you'd feel in their situation. A few kind words or simply listening without judgment can make a huge difference. Empathy may seem difficult, but there are ways to develop it. Here's how:

- **Listen carefully.** When someone tells you about a problem, don't interrupt. Pay attention without thinking about what you'll say next—just be present.

61

- **Ask questions.** Show you care by asking things like, "How do you feel about it?" or "What happened?"

- **Acknowledge emotions.** Reflect back what they might be feeling: "It sounds like you're really upset about this."

- **Don't judge.** Even if you don't understand or agree with their reaction, be supportive instead of critical.

- **Offer help.** Support can be as simple as a reassuring word, a pat on the shoulder, or inviting them to do something fun to take their mind off things.

48. Real Friends Help Each Other

When a friend is struggling, the most important thing is to let them know you're there. You don't need to have all the answers or magically fix their problems. Just listening—even when they're venting about the same thing for the tenth time—can make a huge difference. Of course, if you can also offer practical help, they'll really appreciate it. If they're struggling with homework, offer to study together. If they're going through an emotional rough patch, suggest doing something fun to take their mind off things. Sometimes, grabbing an ice cream together can work wonders.

But be careful: don't give advice unless they ask for it. Most of the time, people just need to talk, not be told what to do. Listening with empathy can be far more helpful than throwing solutions at them. At the end of the day, helping each other is what real friendship is about. You don't have to be perfect or always know the right thing to say. Just being present, listening, and offering support is more than enough. And one day, when you need help, your friend will be there for you too.

49. How to Handle Fights with Friends

Arguing with a friend might feel like the end of the world, but trust me—it's not. Conflicts are normal, especially at your age. Whether it's a misunderstanding, a dumb joke taken the wrong way, or a difference of opinion, fights happen to everyone. The important thing is knowing how to handle them before they turn into massive blowouts. You don't have to turn into the Hulk every time something goes wrong! Stay calm and try to understand your friend's point of view. Here's how to deal with arguments the right way:

- **Don't hold grudges.** Solve the problem as soon as possible—letting it fester will only make things worse.

- **Listen before reacting.** Try to see their perspective instead of jumping straight into attack mode.

- **Stay respectful.** Even if you're mad, avoid yelling or throwing insults—that only makes things worse.

- **Own your mistakes.** If you messed up, admit it. Apologizing doesn't make you weak—it makes you mature.

- **Find a compromise.** It's not always about winning or losing—look for a middle ground.

- **Take a break if needed.** If the argument is getting heated, step away and cool off before talking again.

- **Use humor to lighten the mood.** A well-placed joke (not sarcasm!) can help defuse tension.

50. Bullying

Finally, let's talk about a very serious subject: bullying. It's not just a word you hear at school or on TV—it's a real problem that affects many young people, whether directly or indirectly. Bullying happens when someone is repeatedly targeted, harassed, or humiliated. It can take different forms: physical bullying, like pushing or punching; verbal bullying, like insults and threats; or emotional bullying, like deliberately excluding someone or spreading nasty rumors. And let's not forget cyberbullying, which happens online, often on social media (more on this later). Bullying is a serious problem because it can destroy a person's confidence and self-esteem, sometimes with long-term consequences. Victims often feel isolated, afraid, and powerless. And while bullies might seem strong and dominant, in reality, they're often acting out of their own insecurities and personal issues.

If you are a victim of bullying

First of all, remember that it's not your fault. No one deserves to be bullied. Talk to an adult you trust, like a teacher or parent—don't keep it to yourself. There are people who can help you, but they need to know what's happening. Try to avoid situations where a bully might target you, and never react with violence. Most bullies are looking for a reaction, so stay calm and walk away as soon as you can.

If you see someone being bullied

Don't just look the other way. You don't have to be a superhero, but you can make a big difference just by letting the victim know they're not alone. Report what you see to a trusted adult—staying silent only helps the bully. Doing the right thing can help stop bullying and support the person being targeted.

If you are bullying others

It's hard to admit if you're a bully, but recognizing it is the first step toward change. Ask yourself why you act this way. Many bullies have their own personal struggles that they try to hide by putting others down. If you find yourself bullying others, talk to someone you trust and ask for help. There are better ways to deal with your emotions than hurting others. Kindness and respect will take you much further in life than bullying ever will.

Chapter 6: 10 Mysteries About School and Learning

Can you help me? If you're enjoying this book, I'd truly appreciate it if you could leave a review on Amazon by scanning the following QR code with your smartphone:

For you, it only takes a few seconds, but for me, it's an invaluable help. Thank you in advance! If there's something you don't like or think could be improved, feel free to email me at m.pabst.en@booksgopublications.com. Your feedback helps me make this book even better!

Welcome to Chapter 6, where we dive into school and learning. You'll discover what school is really for and why it's important to find motivation, even on those days when sitting in front of the blackboard feels like a nightmare. We'll explore how to develop a learning method that works for you, with practical strategies to study more efficiently and stay focused. But school isn't the only place where learning happens! We'll also talk about learning in a broader sense—whether it's picking up a hobby, mastering a musical instrument, or excelling in sports.

51. Why School Actually Matters

I know—school can feel like an endless cycle of boring lessons, piles of homework, and waking up way too early. But even if it doesn't seem like it right now, school plays a huge role in your personal growth. First of all, it prepares you for the future. And I don't just mean getting a good job. School teaches you critical thinking, problem-solving, and teamwork skills—things you'll need no matter what you decide to do in life. Whether you dream of becoming an astronaut, a doctor, or a TikTok influencer, a solid education will make everything easier. Another big reason school is important? It helps you understand the world. History classes explain how we got here, science teaches you the laws of nature, and geography introduces you to different countries and cultures. Sure, memorizing dates of world wars might feel pointless, but all this knowledge helps you make smarter decisions in life. And let's not forget friendships. School is one of the best places to make friends and develop social skills. The people you meet here might stick with you for life. Sharing experiences, laughing together in class, and surviving tough teachers creates strong bonds. After all, who else but your classmates can truly understand how unbearable your math teacher is (even though, deep down, he's probably just trying to help you)?

School also helps you discover your passions. Whether you love art, sports, science, or literature, school gives you a chance to explore and figure out what truly excites you. You might develop a love for numbers in math class, or realize how fascinating chemistry can be. Finally, school teaches you discipline and responsibility. Managing homework, meeting deadlines, and taking responsibility for your work are skills that will help you for the rest of your life. So next time you feel like complaining about school, remember—it's more than just a place where you spend your days. It's an investment in your future, a chance to understand the world, a place to make lifelong friends, and an opportunity to discover who you really are.

52. How to Keep Up Motivation at School

Finding the motivation to face school can be very difficult. But don't worry—I've got some simple tips to help you boost your motivation and make school a little more bearable. First of all, think about your future. Yeah, I know—I sound like your parents, but hear me out. Picture yourself with your dream job, traveling the world, or doing something you love. A good education opens doors, not just through grades, but by giving you skills and knowledge that can actually help you achieve your dreams.

Also, find something you genuinely enjoy learning about. Maybe you love science—think about how cool it is to understand how the universe works. If you're into art, use your classes to express yourself. Even if school isn't always exciting, focusing on the subjects that interest you can make a big difference. Finally, reward yourself. When you complete a tough task or reach a goal, treat yourself. Watch an episode of your favorite TV show, play a game, or grab an ice cream. Having something to look forward to makes studying way more bearable. Bottom line: motivation isn't about loving every second of school—it's about finding small ways to keep pushing forward, one step at a time.

53. Learning Methods

Now let's talk about learning methods. I know—just hearing those words might make you yawn, but trust me, having a solid study method can take you from stressed-out panic mode to total confidence. Finding a strategy that works for you is like discovering the ultimate cheat code in your favorite video game—once you've got it, everything becomes easier. A learning method is a set of techniques and strategies that help you absorb and remember information more effectively. Mastering this skill now will not only help you ace tests and exams, but also give you a powerful way to learn for the rest of your life. But here's the thing: not every method works for everyone. That's why it's important to experiment and find what clicks for you. You need to experiment with different techniques and see which one fits you best. However, some techniques are widely known to be effective. Mind maps, for example, are a great tool for organizing and visualizing information. Drawing a mind map helps you see connections between concepts and remember them more easily—it's like creating a roadmap for your brain.

Another effective technique is repeating aloud. When you're reviewing material, try explaining it out loud as if you were teaching someone else. Yes, it might make you feel like you're talking to yourself, but who cares if it works? Taking regular breaks is another essential strategy. Studying for hours without a break is like trying to run a marathon without stopping for water—your brain needs time to recharge. Another tip is breaking down work into smaller parts instead of tackling an entire chapter in one go. This makes studying less overwhelming and helps you see real progress. It's also important to find the right time of day to study. Some people are more focused in the morning, others in the evening. Figure out when your brain is most active and schedule your study sessions accordingly. Don't forget that sleep plays a crucial role—sacrificing rest to study more will only make your brain slower and less efficient. Finally, creating a daily study routine can help keep you consistent. Writing down a schedule, even if it sounds boring, can actually boost your productivity and prevent procrastination. Finding the perfect study method takes experimentation and patience, but once you do, it will make your life so much easier.

54. The Best Places to Study

Not all places are ideal for focus and concentration, so choosing the right study environment can make a huge difference. The library is a classic option—quiet, filled with useful resources, and best of all, no distractions. It's like a temple of knowledge, where you can dive into your books without interruptions. Plus, seeing other people studying can be motivating. It's hard to scroll through Instagram when everyone around you is laser-focused on their work. If you prefer studying in a group, try meeting up with friends who are actually planning to study (not just chat). Find a space where you can all sit together, like a study room or someone's living room. Studying in a group can be incredibly helpful—you can help each other out, exchange ideas, and explain concepts that might be confusing.

Another great place is your own bedroom, but only if you can eliminate distractions. Make sure your desk is organized and that everything you need is within reach. Put your phone on silent or, even better, leave it in another room. Some people also enjoy studying outside, like in a quiet park. A bit of fresh air and natural light can work wonders for concentration. Just make sure you pick a spot that's comfortable and free from distractions.

55. Exam Anxiety

Exam anxiety—what a nightmare! Just hearing the word "exam" can make your stomach knot up and your mind go blank. But here's the truth: a little anxiety is completely normal and can actually help sharpen your focus. The real issue arises when anxiety becomes overwhelming. Fortunately, there are ways to manage it and stay calm under pressure:

- **Repeat aloud to someone.** Grab a friend, a relative, or even your pet, and explain the concepts as if you were teaching them. If your dog doesn't understand physics, at least he won't judge you!

- **Practice relaxation exercises.** Take a few minutes to do deep breathing or short meditations. Inhale deeply, hold for a few seconds, and exhale slowly—this can work wonders in calming your nerves.

- **Put it in perspective.** Instead of seeing it as an insurmountable challenge, remind yourself that in a few years, you probably won't even remember this test. It's just a temporary hurdle, not the end of the world.

- **Plan your revision well.** Break down the syllabus into smaller, manageable parts and review a little each day. This will prevent last-minute panic and make you feel much more in control.

56. School Pressure

Pressure at school can feel overwhelming, especially when you see classmates getting good grades effortlessly while you struggle to keep up. But everyone learns at their own pace—just because someone else seems to grasp things instantly doesn't mean you're not smart. Comparing yourself to others is a dangerous trap that can leave you feeling inadequate. Instead, focus on your own growth. Have you improved over the last few months? Have you learned something new? That's what really matters. Think of school like a race. If you spend all your time looking at other runners, you'll likely trip and fall. But if you focus on your own steps, you'll move forward with confidence. Instead of feeling discouraged by others' success, use it as motivation. Excellence can inspire you rather than make you feel inferior. Maybe you didn't get the highest grade, but you understood a concept you previously struggled with—that's a win!

So, next time you feel crushed by school pressure, take a deep breath. You're not competing with anyone but yourself. Focus on your own progress, and be proud of every step forward. If you must compare yourself to someone, compare yourself to the person you were a few months ago. You'll realize you've come much further than you thought.

57. Hobbies, Music, and Sports

Did you know that learning isn't just something that happens in the classroom? Picking up a hobby, playing a sport, or learning a musical instrument can be just as important for your personal growth—and let's be honest, it's probably way more fun than reviewing math or physics. For example, learning to play a musical instrument doesn't just make you the coolest person in the neighborhood—it also improves coordination, boosts concentration, and sharpens memory skills. Plus, let's not forget, it's a pretty impressive talent that might even amaze your friends. Hobbies are another great way to grow while having fun. Whether it's painting, cycling, cooking, or anything else that excites you, dedicating time to a hobby allows you to explore your interests and develop your talents. It's not just about relaxation and enjoyment—hobbies can also help you learn new skills and gain confidence in yourself.

Sports are in a league of their own. Not only do they keep you in shape, but they also teach teamwork, discipline, and perseverance. Whether you're into volleyball, swimming, or martial arts, playing a sport helps you develop a strong mindset and manage stress more effectively. Plus, it's a fantastic way to make new friends while having fun. Never think of hobbies, music, or sports as a waste of time compared to studying. In fact, balancing your academic work with extracurricular activities helps you become a more well-rounded and balanced person.

58. Figuring Out What You Want to Be

At some point, you've probably started thinking about what you want to do when you grow up. First of all, let me reassure you—nothing is set in stone. You can always change your mind, explore new paths, and discover new passions throughout your life. Even adults switch careers, so don't feel trapped by a choice you make as a teenager. To start figuring out your future career, think about what you enjoy doing in your free time. If you love drawing, maybe a career in art or design could be for you. If you're passionate about technology, you might consider engineering or computer science. Your hobbies and interests can often point you in the right direction. Another great way to explore career options is by talking to people. Ask your parents, teachers, relatives, or older friends about their jobs— what they do, what they love about their work, and what challenges they face. You never know, their experiences might inspire you or introduce you to careers you hadn't even thought about before. And yes, that includes listening to your cousin talk about her job at the bank!

It's also important to try different activities. Participating in internships, workshops, or volunteering can help you get a clearer idea of what you really enjoy. Not sure if you'd like working with kids? Try volunteering at a summer camp. Wondering if you're interested in biology? Try an internship in a lab. Hands-on experience is one of the best ways to discover what truly excites you. Another tip: think about your strengths. If you're great at math, you might consider careers in finance, science, or engineering. If you have excellent communication skills, careers in marketing, journalism, or public relations could be a good fit. Recognizing your strengths will help you identify careers where you can thrive and feel fulfilled. Most importantly—don't stress too much. Finding your dream career takes time. If you don't know exactly what you want to do right now, that's completely okay. Life is a journey, and part of the fun is exploring and discovering new possibilities along the way.

59. Mentors

Let's talk about mentors. A mentor is someone who helps you grow, improve, and become the best version of yourself. They can be parents, teachers, coaches, or anyone who genuinely cares about your development in a specific area. A mentor is someone who has already experienced what you're going through and can offer valuable advice, motivation, and support. Think of a teacher who helps you grasp a complicated subject or a coach who pushes you to give your best in sports. These people aren't just doing a job—they're there to guide, inspire, and sometimes give you a push when you need it most. Mentors help you see things from a different perspective and can steer you away from mistakes they've already learned from. You don't have to look far to find a mentor. It could be your science teacher, who fascinates you with the mysteries of the universe, or your volleyball coach, who teaches you the importance of teamwork. A parent, older sibling, or family member can also be a great mentor, offering support and advice when you need it most. And don't think mentorship is just for teenagers—even adults have mentors. Throughout life, you'll meet different people who inspire and help you grow in new ways. So keep your eyes open for these important figures. Listen to their advice, learn from their experiences, and let them guide you toward becoming your best self.

60. Technology as a Learning Tool

Let's talk about technology and how it can be your secret weapon for learning. The internet and digital tools have completely transformed education. In the past, if you wanted to learn something new, you had to go to the library, flip through dusty books, and hope to find the right answer. Today, with just a few clicks, you can access almost any information instantly. It's like carrying a giant encyclopedia in your pocket—without the dust! Thanks to the internet, you can find videos, articles, and interactive tutorials on almost any subject. Want to understand the theory of relativity? There are animated explanations and expert lectures to guide you. Need to style your hair for a formal event? YouTube has step-by-step video tutorials. And let's not forget the educational apps that turn your phone into a personal tutor. With the right approach, technology can be your greatest ally in education. But like everything, technology has its downsides. One major risk is misinformation—not everything you find online is true. So, it's crucial to verify sources and cross-check information. If you're unsure, ask a teacher or someone knowledgeable. Another issue is cheating—with so many tools available, it's easy to copy answers, let AI write your essays, or shortcut assignments. But in reality, cheating only hurts you. One day, when you actually need to use that knowledge, taking the easy way out won't help. Technology is a powerful tool, but only if you use it wisely and responsibly. We'll explore its impact in more detail later, but for now, remember to use it as a way to boost your learning—not replace it.

Chapter 7: 10 Mysteries of Addiction

Addictions aren't just about drugs. Some things that are harmless in the right doses—like video games, social media, and even food—can also become addictions. It's essential not to fall into the trap of addiction, as it can negatively impact every aspect of your life: your health, relationships, school, and future in general. In this chapter, we'll explore the main addictions you need to watch out for. You'll also find tips on how to recognize, avoid, and cope with them.

61. Dopamine: The Root of All Addictions

Dopamine is a neurotransmitter, meaning it helps neurons—your brain's nerve cells—communicate with each other. Its job is to generate positive feelings and a sense of well-being. That's why, like serotonin, it's often called the "happiness hormone." You know that amazing feeling you get when you play sports or eat a delicious ice cream? You can thank dopamine. It's essential for survival because it motivates you to do things that are good for you, like eating, exercising, and socializing. The problem is that your brain loves dopamine a little too much and can become overly attached to activities that produce it. When you do something that releases a big dopamine hit, your brain thinks: "That felt great! I want to do that again!" And that's where the trouble starts.

Addictions develop when the brain starts constantly craving dopamine from a specific activity[11]. Whether it's junk food, social media, shopping, alcohol, or drugs, all of these can trick your brain into believing they're essential to happiness. The issue is that the more dopamine your brain gets from these sources, the more it wants—leading to addiction. Activities that release dopamine start to take priority over everything else, and before you

---

[11] **Wise, R., & Robble, M. A. (2020).** *Dopamine and Addiction.* Annual Review of Psychology, 71, 79-106.

know it, you might be neglecting school, friendships, or even your health just to chase that feeling of pleasure. Understanding dopamine and its role in addiction can help you stay in control. You can still enjoy the things you love, but in moderation. And remember—real happiness doesn't just come from dopamine rushes, but from maintaining a healthy, fulfilling balance in your life.

62. Cigarettes

Smoking isn't just a bad habit—it's one of the fastest ways to ruin your health, weaken your athletic performance, and even harm the environment. As you probably already know, smoking is terrible for your body. Every time you light a cigarette, you inhale over 7,000 chemicals, at least 70 of which are carcinogenic. Yes, you read that right—carcinogenic. Smoking can lead to a whole host of health issues, including lung cancer, heart disease, strokes, and severe respiratory problems. Not exactly the "cool" image you want to project, is it? And it's not just your problem. Secondhand smoke—the smoke inhaled by people around you—is just as dangerous. If you smoke, you're putting your friends, family, and even pets at risk. On top of that, smoking is terrible for the environment. Every cigarette you smoke releases toxins into the air, and cigarette butts are one of the hardest types of waste to dispose of. They end up in rivers, oceans, and parks, polluting the environment and harming both plants and animals.

Quitting smoking is tough, especially if you start young. Nicotine is highly addictive, and your brain quickly starts craving more and more of it. Every attempt to quit is met with withdrawal symptoms, making it a difficult cycle to break. That's why the best decision is to never start in the first place. Smoking just to fit in with others is one of the worst choices you can make. There's nothing cool about harming yourself to impress people. On the contrary, it's much cooler to be the one who chooses not to smoke—someone who values their health and sets a positive example for others. And what about e-cigarettes? They might seem like a "safer" alternative, but they also contain harmful chemicals that can damage your lungs and lead to addiction. Make the smart choice. Choose health. Choose to be different. Choose not to smoke.

63. Alcohol

Have you ever had a beer or a glass of wine? I'm not here to lecture you—a drink now and then isn't a crime—but when you overdo it, especially at your age, it can lead to some seriously unpleasant situations. First of all, alcohol acts as a depressant on the brain, slowing down cognitive and motor functions. This means that while you might feel like the king of the world after a few drinks, in reality, you're becoming less coordinated and less in control. This can lead to embarrassing moments, dangerous situations, and, in the worst cases, serious accidents—which is why drinking and driving is absolutely forbidden. A teenager's body is still developing, and alcohol can have much more harmful effects than it does on an adult. Excessive drinking at a young age can interfere with brain development and significantly increase the risk of addiction later in life. Beyond that, alcohol abuse can lead to severe health issues, including liver disease, heart problems, and a whole range of other complications.

I'm not saying you should never drink. A glass of wine at dinner or a beer with friends isn't the end of the world. But it must be done in moderation and with responsibility. Most importantly, you should wait until you're legally allowed to drink. If you do decide to drink, know your limits, and don't feel pressured just because others are doing it. Making smart choices now will help you stay in control of your future.

64. Cannabis

Now let's talk about cannabis and the habit of smoking it. Have you ever seen your friends rolling those famous "joints"? Cannabis contains THC, the chemical that makes you feel high. It may sound like fun, but it has serious negative effects on your developing brain. For teenagers, smoking or using cannabis can impair memory, concentration, and learning. It can also affect your ability to make decisions—which isn't exactly ideal when you're trying to figure out what you want to do with your life. Smoking cannabis, like smoking cigarettes, is also harmful to your lungs. It can cause respiratory problems, chronic bronchitis, and other long-term lung damage. What's more, regular cannabis use can lead to psychological dependence, making it seem impossible to relax or have fun without it.

So how do you stay away from joints? First of all, learn to say "no." You don't have to accept a joint just because everyone else is smoking. Remember, saying no doesn't make you less cool—it makes you smarter. Find other ways to deal with stress and have fun. Sports, music, hobbies, and even video games (in moderation) can be great ways to unwind without damaging your brain. Talk to someone you trust. If you're tempted to try cannabis, speak to an adult or a friend. Sometimes, just discussing it can help you see things from a different perspective and make better decisions. Finally, do some research on the real effects of cannabis and tobacco, beyond what I've just mentioned. The more you understand how harmful they can be, the less likely you'll be to give in to curiosity or social pressure.

65. Hard Drugs

Let's talk about "hard" drugs—the substances that are the fastest way to destroy your life. Hard drugs are pure evil. Cocaine, heroin, methamphetamine, ecstasy—these are all names to be avoided at all costs. Hard drugs are extremely dangerous because they create devastating dependencies and have long-term negative effects on both the body and mind. Cocaine can cause serious heart problems and permanent brain damage. Heroin can lead to death by overdose. Methamphetamines can literally destroy brain tissue, causing severe memory and behavioral disorders. Ecstasy can cause irreversible brain and heart damage. It's essential to stay away from these substances to protect your life and the lives of those around you. Not only do hard drugs ruin those who use them, but they also destroy the lives of family and friends. Watching a loved one fall into the downward spiral of hard drugs is a devastating experience that I wouldn't wish on anyone.

If you ever find yourself in a situation where someone offers you these drugs, the right answer is always a resounding "no." There's nothing cool about risking your life for a high. On the contrary, it takes much more strength and intelligence to say "no" and make healthy choices. If you see people around you using hard drugs, report them. You're not a snitch if you do—you're saving lives. Above all, stay away from people who use drugs. It's better to be considered uncool than to put your life at risk.

66. Compulsive Shopping

Shopping is a passion shared by many young women like you, and for many, it's about much more than just buying clothes. Shopping can be a way to express yourself, develop your personal style, and boost your confidence. It's also a great opportunity to spend time with friends, have fun, and relieve everyday stress. So, there's nothing wrong with enjoying a little shopping every now and then. However, in some cases, shopping can turn into an addiction with negative consequences. Compulsive shopping disorder, also known as oniomania, is a behavioral condition in which a person feels an irresistible urge to shop excessively, often buying things they don't need or can't afford[12]. This disorder can lead to serious financial, emotional, and relationship problems. It's not always easy to recognize when shopping becomes a problem, but there are key warning signs. If you shop to improve your mood, even when you don't actually need anything, or if you buy things but never use them, you might be struggling with oniomania. Other warning signs include lying about your purchases, accumulating debt, or feeling guilty after shopping too much. If shopping starts to interfere with your daily life or relationships because you're constantly thinking about it, that's a clear red flag.

To prevent or overcome compulsive shopping, there are several strategies you can try. Start by setting a monthly budget for your purchases and sticking to it. When you go out, bring only a limited amount of cash and leave your bank cards at home. Instead of shopping as a way to handle stress, find healthier alternatives like sports, meditation, or creative hobbies. Avoid browsing online stores or window shopping without a clear purpose. If you do need to shop, make a list in advance and stick to it. Another useful trick is to wait at least 24 hours before making a big purchase—this gives you time to decide if it's really necessary. If you feel like you can't control your shopping habits, consider talking to your parents or a trusted family member. Seeking help from a psychologist or therapist can also be a great step toward understanding and overcoming compulsive shopping.

---

[12] **Pazarlis, P., Katsigiannopoulos, K., Papazisis, G., Bolimou, S., & Garyfallos, G. (2008).** *Compulsive buying: a review.* Annals of General Psychiatry, 7(1).

67. Social Networks, the Internet, and TV

These days, social networks, the Internet, and even television are powerful tools. You can learn a lot from the comfort of your own home, connect with friends all over the world, and discover things you never thought possible. But, like everything else, they also have their negative side. And I'm not just talking about tasteless memes. The Internet, social networks, and television can become real addictions, stealing your precious time and making you lose touch with reality. Have you ever opened Instagram just to check a notification and suddenly found yourself watching cat videos for an hour? Or have you ever binge-watched an entire season of a new series in one sitting? Okay, it can happen to anyone, even adults. But if it happens too often, you may have a problem. To prevent the Internet, TV, and social networks from becoming an addiction, here are a few tips:

- **Set time limits.** Use your phone's settings to restrict the time you spend on apps and set designated periods when you can't watch TV. It may sound extreme, but it's very effective.

- **Take breaks from technology.** Every once in a while, disconnect completely. Turn off your phone and TV, and go for a walk, read a book, or talk to someone face-to-face. The real world is much more interesting than you think.

- **Clean up your networks.** Only follow people and pages that inspire you and make you happy. If an account makes you feel inadequate or stressed, unfollow it. The Internet is full of content, so don't waste your time consuming things that make you feel bad!

- **Use the Internet to learn.** Try to balance idle time spent on social networks or TV with more productive online activities, such as taking courses, reading interesting articles, or watching documentaries.

68. Food

We've already talked about eating disorders, so I won't go into detail. However, I'd like to remind you that food can also become an addiction. Yes, even delicious potato chips can turn into your worst enemy if you overindulge. Obesity isn't just a matter of weight; it's a serious health issue that can lead to conditions like diabetes and cardiovascular diseases. It's easy to fall into the trap of junk food. All it takes is a moment of boredom, stress, or sadness to reach for your favorite snack. The problem is that junk food is designed to be irresistible—loaded with sugars and fats that trigger a flood of dopamine in your brain. You feel good for a short while, but then you crave more. Here are a few simple tips to prevent food from becoming an addiction:

- **Don't keep junk food at home.** If it's not easily accessible, you won't be tempted to overeat.

- **Eat when you're actually hungry—not out of boredom or stress.** Learn to distinguish real hunger from emotional eating. If you're feeling bored or stressed, find a different way to cope—go for a walk, read a book, or call a friend.

- **Stay active.** Regular exercise helps you manage your weight and improves your mood. Find a sport or physical activity you enjoy and make it part of your routine.

69. Video Games

Do you love video games? While many people assume that gaming is more popular among boys, the truth is that plenty of teenage girls love video games too. But like anything else, video games can become a problem if they're overused. Yes, even gaming can be addictive. If you play too much, it's easy to lose track of time and start neglecting important activities like studying, sleeping, and even spending time with friends and family. Video game addiction happens when you struggle to stop playing, even when you know you should be doing something else. If you find yourself skipping meals, losing sleep, or avoiding real-life social interactions just to keep playing, gaming may be turning into a problem.

To avoid this, set limits on how much time you spend gaming. Decide in advance—ideally with your parents—how much time per week you want to dedicate to video games, and stick to that limit. Use timers or apps to help track your gaming time. And most importantly, make sure you've finished your homework and responsibilities before turning on your console. Think of video games as a reward for completing important tasks—not something that gets in the way of them. If you feel like video games are taking over your life, don't hesitate to talk to a friend, family member, or trusted adult. Sometimes, an outside perspective can help you see things more clearly and regain a healthy balance.

70. Gambling

Finally, let's talk about gambling—an activity that might seem exciting and fun at first, but can quickly spiral into a serious addiction. Gambling isn't just about placing big bets in casinos—it also includes sports betting, online gaming, slot machines, and lotteries. Even something as seemingly harmless as a slot machine can turn into a major problem if not handled responsibly. Gambling addiction happens when you start betting money you can't afford to lose. At first, it may seem like just a fun way to win (or more often, lose) a little cash, but over time, you might find yourself caught in a dangerous cycle known as "ludopathy". Every time you lose, you may feel the urge to keep playing to win back what you lost. And every time you win, you might want to chase that adrenaline rush again as soon as possible. This behavior can lead to serious financial trouble. People with gambling addictions often spend all their money on bets, neglecting important expenses and, in some cases, accumulating debt.

Gambling can also damage relationships. Many gambling addicts lie to their friends and family about how much time and money they've spent gambling, which creates tension, conflict, and trust issues. The scary part is that gambling is often seen as a normal and socially acceptable activity, making it harder to recognize when it's becoming a real problem. To avoid falling into gambling addiction, the best advice is not to start at all—especially at your age, when it's not even legal to gamble! If you ever feel that gambling is becoming a problem, talk to someone you trust. It can be difficult to admit you need help, but reaching out is the first and most important step toward recovery.

Chapter 8: 10 Mysteries of the Internet, Social Media, and Technology

The Internet, social media, and technology have become an integral part of modern life. After all, the opportunities they offer are endless, and it would be foolish not to take advantage of them. But, as Spider-Man so wisely said, "With great power comes great responsibility." This chapter explores the wonders and the dangers of the digital world, helping you navigate the Internet, social media, and technology wisely.

71. The Pros and Cons of the Internet

The Internet has transformed the world in ways our grandparents could never have imagined. Just think how easy it is today to find answers to your strangest questions or learn new skills through an online course. Want to learn to play the guitar, bake a cake, or even build a rocket? Okay, maybe not the rocket, but almost everything else is just a click away. One of the greatest advantages of the Internet is access to an enormous amount of information. You can learn practically anything quickly and for free (or almost). Online courses, YouTube tutorials, articles, and millions of books are available to everyone. This makes education more accessible than ever. No matter where you live or what resources you have at your disposal, the Internet can open the doors to a world of knowledge.

But the Internet also comes with risks. One of the biggest dangers is fake news. In the vast ocean of available information, not everything is reliable. It's easy to come across false or misleading information that can shape your thoughts and decisions. That's why it's essential to learn how to distinguish trustworthy sources from hoaxes. Another major concern is the loss of privacy. Every time you share something online, you leave a digital footprint. Your personal information can be collected and used in ways you might not even realize. It's important to be aware of what you're sharing and with whom. Additionally, social media can often become a toxic environment, where cyberbullying thrives. People hide behind anonymity and say things they would never dare to say in person. This can make the online world stressful and even harmful to mental health. Finally, as we've discussed before, there's the risk of Internet addiction. Spending too much time online can negatively impact real-life relationships, productivity, and well-being.

72. The Pros and Cons of Social Media

Social media has transformed the world we live in. Today, you can stay connected with friends across the globe, share moments of your life in real time, and even become famous thanks to a viral video. Social networks are also a great way to stay updated on current events and express yourself creatively. Whether it's showcasing your talents, engaging in discussions, or simply sharing your daily life, social media offers endless opportunities to connect and interact with others. However, social media also has a dark side. One of the biggest risks is oversharing—posting embarrassing or overly personal content. Remember, what you post on the internet stays there forever. Even if you delete a photo or message, someone may have already saved or shared it. Think twice before posting anything that could come back to haunt you in the future.

Another issue is comparison. What you see on social media rarely reflects reality. People tend to showcase only the best moments of their lives, creating an illusion of perfection. Don't be fooled by these curated images—behind every polished post is a person dealing with the same struggles, insecurities, and challenges as everyone else. If your life doesn't look like the glamorous ones you see online, don't stress—nobody's life is actually perfect. Lastly, never measure your happiness by the number of likes, followers, or comments you receive. Social media can trick you into thinking that your worth depends on your popularity, but the truth is very different. True self-esteem comes from meaningful relationships and real-life experiences, not from virtual validation.

73. Online Privacy

Let's talk about online privacy—something that might not seem exciting but is actually crucial. Surfing the web without protecting your privacy is like walking around naked: you're exposing things you should be keeping private! Every time you post a photo, send a message, or even do a simple Google search, you leave digital traces behind. This data can be collected, analyzed, and used in ways you might not expect. Think twice before sharing anything personal online. Never post sensitive information like your home address, phone number, or—especially—financial details such as your credit card number. Even seemingly harmless details can be misused, so be cautious about what you put out there.

Also, avoid sharing anything too intimate or embarrassing that could come back to haunt you in the future. A good rule of thumb: if you wouldn't want your parents, teachers, or future employer to see it, don't post it. To protect your accounts, use strong, unique passwords for each one and enable two-factor authentication whenever possible—it's an extra layer of security that can prevent hacking. Lastly, take a few minutes to check and adjust your social media privacy settings. Many platforms allow you to control who can see your posts and personal information. It's a small effort that can make a huge difference in keeping your data safe.

74. Online Security

More and more people fall victim to online scams every day. Surfing the internet without proper precautions is like walking into a dark alley with a T-shirt that says, "Steal from me." First, always be cautious about who's messaging you. If you receive strange messages from strangers—or even friends that seem out of the ordinary—be wary. Hackers often hijack accounts to scam others. If a message seems suspicious, verify it by reaching out to the person through another means of communication. Online scams, like phishing, are extremely common. Phishing is when fraudsters try to steal personal information, such as passwords or credit card details, by pretending to be a trusted company. They often send emails or messages that look like they're from your bank or a service you use. Never click on suspicious links or enter personal data unless you're certain the request is legitimate. If an email asks you to update your details, don't click the link. Instead, go directly to the official website by typing the address into your browser.

Avoid downloading files from sketchy sources, and only browse trusted sites. Always check a website's reliability before downloading anything. Keeping your operating system and antivirus software updated is crucial—updates often contain security patches that protect against new threats. Think of them like vaccines for your computer. When shopping online or accessing sensitive information, use secure connections. Public Wi-Fi networks are vulnerable to hackers, so avoid using them for anything that involves financial data. If you must, consider using a VPN to encrypt your data and protect your privacy (you can Google what a VPN is). Lastly, trust your instincts. If something seems too good to be true, it probably is. If an online offer looks suspicious, avoid it. You won't lose anything by skipping a fake "golden opportunity," but you might lose a lot if you take the bait.

75. Fake News

"Fake news" refers to misleading or completely false information that is deliberately spread to deceive, manipulate, or profit from misinformation. You might think spotting fake news is easy, but it's not always that simple. Some fake stories are so absurd that they're obviously false—like a cat that learned to drive a car. But other fake news articles are much more deceptive, blending real facts with false information to create a convincing but misleading narrative. It's not always a simple case of truth versus lies; sometimes, fake news exists in a gray area, making it even harder to identify. Some misinformation is designed to make you believe things that aren't true. Others are straight-up scams—like articles that promise you easy money if you click on a suspicious link or give out personal information.

To avoid falling for fake news, it's important to develop a healthy skepticism. Don't blindly believe everything you read online. Always verify the source of the information. If something sounds strange or too sensational to be true, there's probably a catch. Check if multiple reputable sources are reporting the same news. If a trusted news site isn't mentioning it, that's a red flag. Be especially cautious with information that spreads through social media. Social networks are a breeding ground for misinformation, as viral content often plays on emotions to spread quickly. If a post makes you extremely angry, amused, or sad, pause and think before reacting. Fake news often has shocking headlines and dramatic images to grab your attention. Before sharing anything, read it carefully, verify the context, and make sure it's accurate. Don't contribute to the problem by spreading misinformation.

76. Cyberbullying

Cyberbullying is an ugly beast. Unlike traditional bullying, cyberbullying takes place online, where perpetrators hide behind screens and keyboards. Many cyberbullies say or do cruel things online that they would never have the courage to say or do in person. The internet, for some reason, can bring out the worst in people. Cyberbullying comes in many forms: hateful comments, private message threats, spreading false rumors, or even sharing embarrassing photos or videos without permission. Just because it happens in the digital world doesn't mean it's not serious—its impact on victims is very real and can be devastating.

If you are a victim of cyberbullying

If you're being cyberbullied, the most important thing is not to respond. Instead, report the incident to the platform where it occurred. Social networks are aware of the issue and often have tools to report harassment, which can lead to the bully being banned. Keep records of the harassment—take screenshots of messages or comments—and talk to a trusted adult, such as a parent, teacher, or school counselor. Depending on how serious the situation is, reporting the incident to the authorities may also be necessary.

If you witness cyberbullying

If you see someone being cyberbullied, don't just ignore it. Support the victim, report the behavior to platform moderators, and encourage them to talk to a trusted adult. Sometimes, just letting the victim know they're not alone can make a huge difference.

If you are a cyberbully

And what if you realize that you're the one engaging in cyberbullying? Stop immediately and think about what you're doing. Ask yourself why you feel the need to hurt others, and try talking to someone about how you feel. Many times, cyberbullying comes from insecurities or personal struggles. Getting help can allow you to resolve these issues in a healthier way—without hurting others in the process.

77. Revenge Porn

Revenge porn is one of the most serious and devastating forms of cyberbullying. But what exactly does it mean? It refers to the online sharing of intimate images or videos ("nudes" or "sex tapes") of a person without their consent, often as an act of revenge after a breakup. The term itself explains it: "revenge" means getting back at someone—but in this case, in an incredibly harmful and cruel way. The consequences of revenge porn are extreme. Victims often experience shame, anxiety, and depression, and in some cases, the emotional distress is so severe that it has led to suicide. Once intimate images are shared online, it's almost impossible to erase them completely. The humiliation and trauma can haunt a person for years, affecting their mental health, relationships, and even career opportunities.

That's why you should never send intimate photos or videos of yourself to anyone—not even someone you trust. It might seem fun or romantic in the moment, but once it's out of your hands, you lose control over it. There's no way to guarantee that the person you sent it to won't share it or lose it, even unintentionally. If you ever receive an intimate photo or video from someone, delete it immediately. Do not keep it, and never, ever share it. Distributing private images without consent is not just morally wrong—it's also a crime in many countries. It's important to never treat this issue as a joke and to raise awareness among your friends. Talk to them about the devastating consequences of revenge porn for victims. This is not just gossip—it's a serious crime that can ruin lives. Protect yourself, be responsible, and help put an end to this dangerous practice.

78. Artificial Intelligence

Artificial intelligence, or AI for short, is one of the most powerful and revolutionary tools of our time. Just a few years ago, the idea of intelligent machines learning, making decisions, and even driving cars seemed like pure science fiction. Now, it's becoming a reality. AI is transforming everything—from medicine and finance to entertainment and education. It can help you find answers to complex questions, suggest new learning methods, and even assist in creating digital art or music. The possibilities are enormous, and AI has the potential to make life easier in countless ways.

However, like any powerful tool, AI comes with risks, especially for teenagers. One of the biggest dangers is using AI to cheat or plagiarize. Imagine having an assistant do all your homework for you—sounds tempting, right? But here's the problem: if you let AI do everything, what do you actually learn? Nothing. You miss the opportunity to develop your own skills, critical thinking, and problem-solving abilities. School isn't just about memorizing facts; it's about learning how to think, analyze, and grow. Using AI as a shortcut to avoid doing the work yourself will only hurt you in the long run. AI should be a tool to support your learning, not a replacement for your effort and personal growth.

79. Online Video Games

We've already talked about video games and the risk of addiction, but now let's focus on online gaming. These types of games connect you with people from all over the world. Playing with strangers can be incredibly fun, and in some cases, it can even help you make new friends. However, there are also risks you need to be aware of. One of the biggest dangers in online gaming is security. When you play online, you're interacting with people you don't really know—and that can be dangerous. While some players may be other teenagers, others could be scammers, predators, or people with bad intentions. That's why you should never share personal information such as your real name, address, phone number, or banking details. To stay safe, always keep your personal information private. Use a pseudonym that doesn't reveal your real identity, and make sure your game's privacy settings are as secure as possible. If something feels off, trust your instincts and stop playing with that person.

Another major risk in online gaming is cyberbullying and harassment. Unfortunately, some players use video games as a platform for toxic behavior. If someone starts insulting you, pressuring you, or acting inappropriately, don't hesitate to block and report them. Never ignore bad behavior—even if it's "just a game." Lastly, be careful about financial risks. Many online video games offer microtransactions for things like gadgets, upgrades, and accessories. If you're not careful, you could end up spending a lot of money without realizing it. To avoid this, set spending limits, and if you're using a parent's credit card, always ask for permission first. By being aware of these risks, you can enjoy online gaming safely and responsibly while avoiding unnecessary problems.

80. Balancing Online and Offline Time

We live in a world where being constantly connected has become the norm. Between the internet, social networks, video games, and endless streaming services, it's easy to spend hours glued to a screen. But is this good for your health? Of course not! Balancing your time online and offline is essential for maintaining a healthy and happy life. Research shows that excessive screen time can negatively impact both physical and mental health[13]. Staring at screens for too long strains your eyes, weakens your posture, and overloads your brain with information. More importantly, being online all the time can isolate you from real-life experiences, causing you to miss out on adventures, friendships, and personal growth. The world outside of screens has so much to offer—don't let it pass you by! Here are some practical tips to help you balance your time online and offline:

- **Limit your screen time.** Set a daily limit for how much time you spend online and stick to it. You can use apps that track screen usage to help you manage your digital habits.

- **Plan offline activities.** Make time for things like sports, reading, or hobbies. Having planned activities helps break the cycle of constant screen use.

---

[13] **Hökby, S., Hadlaczky, G., Westerlund, J., Wasserman, D., Balázs, J., Germanavicius, A., Machín, N., Meszaros, G., Sarchiapone, M., Värnik, A., Varnik, P., Westerlund, M., & Carli, V. (2016).** *Are Mental Health Effects of Internet Use Attributable to the Web-Based Content or Perceived Consequences of Usage? A Longitudinal Study of European Adolescents.* JMIR Mental Health, 3.

- **Create tech-free zones at home.** Designate areas like your bedroom or dining room where technology is off-limits. This encourages better sleep and real-life connections with family.

- **Set offline goals.** Challenge yourself to finish a book, improve in a sport, or develop a new skill. Achieving personal milestones will motivate you to unplug more often.

Chapter 9: 10 Mysteries of Independence and Responsibility

Welcome to Chapter 9, where we're going to talk about independence and responsibility. I know these words may sound a little boring to you, but believe me, they're very important. Being independent means taking control of your life, making wise choices and accepting the consequences of your actions with maturity. It's about learning to stand on your own two feet, whether it's managing your time, handling money, or making important decisions without constantly relying on others. Being responsible, on the other hand, means earning the respect of others and proving that you can manage your life without your parents constantly on your back. It's not about being perfect but about showing that you can be trusted. The more responsible you are, the more freedom you'll have. Let's take a look at a few key concepts you should start to understand as you grow into a more independent person.

81. Rights and Responsibilities

As you grow up and move toward adulthood, you enter a world where rights and responsibilities go hand in hand. Having rights means that you benefit from freedoms and protections guaranteed by law, while having responsibilities means that you have duties to fulfill and must be accountable for your actions. For example, you have the right to express your opinion, choose your career path, and decide your place in society. However, you also have the duty to treat others with respect and to fulfill obligations—even when you don't feel like it.

When you start working, you have the right to be paid for your labor, but you also have the duty to be punctual and professional (yes, even when you'd rather stay in bed!). When it comes to voting, you have the right to choose your political representatives, but also the duty to educate yourself on their policies before making an informed decision. No one expects you to become a fully responsible adult overnight—it's a transition, like learning to drive. At first, you practice with guidance, then, as you gain confidence, you take control on your own. Learning to balance your rights and responsibilities is essential for living in harmony with others and being seen as a reliable, valuable person.

82. Learning to Make Decisions

One of the best things about becoming an adult is being able to make your own decisions. Yes, you can finally choose for yourself without always having to ask permission. Want ice cream for breakfast? Yes, you can. Want to dye your hair blue? You can. I'm not suggesting you eat ice cream for breakfast and dye your hair blue, of course! The fact is, making your own decisions is a fundamental part of becoming an independent adult. At first, making decisions can seem a little daunting. You may think, "What if I make the wrong choice?" Don't worry, it's normal to have doubts and make mistakes. These mistakes are part of the learning process; everyone makes mistakes along the way. Here are some practical tips for learning how to make decisions:

- **Get informed.** When you have to make an important decision, gather all the information you can. Talk to people who have experience in the field, do some online research, and try to understand your options. The more you know, the better prepared you'll be to make an informed choice.

- **Weigh up the pros and cons.** Make a mental (or written, if you prefer) list of the pros and cons of each option. This will help you see things more clearly and understand which is the best choice for you.

- **Listen to your instincts.** Sometimes, even after rationally weighing up all the information, your instinct can push you in the right direction. If something seems wrong, your instincts may be right.

- **Don't be afraid to ask for advice.** Talk to trusted friends, family, or mentors. They can offer you different perspectives and help you see things from another angle.

- **Accept that not all your decisions will be good ones.** Some choices will lead to fantastic results, others to unexpected consequences. The mystery is to make sure that every decision, good or bad, teaches you something useful for the future.

83. Developing Practical Skills for Everyday Life

Imagine waking up one day and realizing you have to handle everything on your own. No one to cook for you, no one to wash the dishes, no one to do the grocery shopping. Sounds a little scary, right? That's why learning practical life skills is like having a superpower—it gives you independence and prepares you to take on the world (or at least your own apartment). Let's start with cooking. Knowing how to prepare a decent meal is essential. You don't need to be the next Gordon Ramsay, but you should be able to make more than just toast. Start with simple recipes—like pasta with tomato sauce, grilled chicken, or a fresh salad. You can find easy tutorials on YouTube or ask your parents to teach you a few basics.

Keeping your home clean and organized might seem like a boring chore, but it's something you'll need to know how to do. Start with small daily habits: make your bed every morning, wash the dishes after eating, and vacuum once a week. Breaking down cleaning tasks into small steps makes them much easier to manage and prevents your space from turning into a total mess. Basic household maintenance is another important skill. You don't need to be an expert, but knowing how to use a screwdriver, hang a picture, or inflate a bike tire will save you a lot of time and frustration. And once again, YouTube is your best friend—there are thousands of tutorials for every little household problem you can imagine. These are just a few basic life skills I recommend you start practicing—even if you make mistakes at first. The truth is, one day you'll have to handle all of this on your own, so it's best to start learning now, little by little. Trust me, your future self will thank you!

84. Money Management

When it comes to money, the first thing to understand is that money has value. It doesn't grow on trees or magically appear in your wallet. Every dollar you have in your pocket has been hard-earned, so it's important to learn how to manage it carefully. Managing your money means knowing how much you earn (or receive from your parents), how much you spend, and how much you save each month. So start by recognizing your income and expenses. How much money do you receive each month? It could be pocket money, a part-time job, or other sources of income. Next, list your expenses. There are fixed expenses, such as your phone bill, and variable expenses, such as food, clothing, and money spent on outings with friends.

Then write down how much money you receive and how much you spend each month, and divide up the money you spend into different areas. If you find that you're spending too much in one area, try to cut down on unnecessary spending. For example, maybe you can avoid buying a fourth pair of the same brand of sneakers! Saving money is just as important. You don't need to set aside huge sums at your age, but try to save something every month. Simply setting aside a small percentage of your monthly income can make a big difference over time. Having savings gives you security and allows you to deal with unexpected expenses without stress. Finally, try to avoid debt. It's easy to fall into the trap of spending money you don't have. If you can't afford something, it's better to wait and save rather than go into debt, for example by borrowing money from friends.

85. Complying with the Law

Respecting the law may seem obvious, but it's surprising how often people forget to do it, especially when they think they can get away with it. First of all, you need to understand why laws exist. Laws are there to protect you and others. They're like the rules of a game: without them, chaos would reign supreme. Imagine a basketball match without rules—it would be a total mess. Likewise, life without laws would be a disaster. I know it sounds boring, but it's important to at least know the basic laws. That means you can't steal, vandalize public property, or do other stupid things just because it's fun. The negative consequences can be serious: hefty fines, community service, or, worse, jail time. It's certainly not the best way to impress your friends.

Respect for the law is also a matter of personal integrity. It's not just about avoiding illegal actions, but also about doing the right thing even when no one is watching. For example, if you find a wallet on the street, hand it over to the police instead of keeping it. This not only shows that you respect the law, but also that you respect others. If your friends get into trouble and break the law, don't feel obliged to follow them. It's not cool to be arrested or to have a criminal record. On the contrary, having the courage to say no and do the right thing is much more respectable. If your friends pressure you, remember that real friends would never force you to do something wrong or illegal.

86. Setting Personal Goals

Defining personal goals is one of the most important things you can do to give your life direction. Not having goals is like wandering aimlessly in a video game—it's fun for a while, but in the long run, you get bored. Goals help you focus on what truly matters to you and give you a strong reason to get up in the morning (besides breakfast, of course).

But what does it really mean to set personal goals? It's about thinking ahead—where do you want to be in five or ten years? What do you want to accomplish in life? Your goals can be anything: becoming a computer expert, learning to play guitar like a rock star, or simply striving to become a better person. Goals give you a roadmap to the future you want. One of the greatest benefits of setting goals is the motivation they provide. When you know you're working toward something meaningful, it pushes you to give your best. Plus, achieving your goals brings great satisfaction and boosts your self-esteem. Here are some practical tips for setting your personal goals:

- **Start with long-term goals.** Picture the life you want in five or ten years. Write these goals down in a journal or on a piece of paper. Then break them down into smaller, achievable steps. For example, if you want to become a computer expert, you could start by taking an online course or reading books on the subject.

- **Once you've set long-term goals, define medium and short-term goals.** These are the smaller steps that will bring you closer to the big picture. If your dream is to master the guitar, a medium-term goal might be to learn an entire song, while a short-term goal could be to practice for 30 minutes a day.

- **Turn these goals into daily habits.** Habits are the key to achieving anything. If you can make progress part of your daily routine, you'll reach your goals much faster than you think.

87. Time Management

Managing your time is a bit like being a Jedi master—you need to find the "right balance" between school, friends, hobbies, and all the other activities filling up your life. Time is a precious and limited resource, so knowing how to manage it well can make the difference between feeling overwhelmed and reaching your goals with ease. Organizing your time effectively means planning your days and prioritizing what's truly important. You can't spend all day on Instagram and then complain that you have no time left for homework!

That's why planning is essential. It helps you understand what you need to do and when. Make a list of tasks and prioritize them. What are the most important things you need to complete today? What can wait until tomorrow? Learn to focus on activities that bring you closer to your goals. One of the biggest enemies of time management is procrastination—that little voice inside you saying, "I'll do it later." It's very persuasive, but don't let it fool you. Procrastination only leads to stress and last-minute panic. Tackle important tasks right away, and you'll feel much better instantly.

88. Helping Others

Helping others is one of the secrets to a happy and fulfilling life. Yes, you read that right—helping others gives you a sense of purpose and satisfaction that few other things can. Plus, it's a great way to make new friends and feel part of a community. When you support someone—whether a friend, a family member, or even a stranger—you create a positive impact on their life. Volunteering, for example, is a fantastic way to contribute to society. Many organizations need extra hands, from soup kitchens and hospitals to environmental groups and animal shelters. Find something that speaks to you and get involved. Not only will you be making a difference, but you'll also learn new skills and meet amazing people.

Even outside of volunteering, there are endless ways to help others in daily life. You can lend a hand at home by taking on small chores without being asked, assist a friend in solving a problem, or simply practice kindness toward those around you. A smile, a kind word, or a small gesture can brighten someone's day more than you might realize. Helping others also allows you to see the world from different perspectives, making you more empathetic and aware of other people's struggles. It helps you grow as a person and develop a deeper sense of compassion.

89. Environmental Responsibilities

Every action we take leaves an ecological footprint—a fancy way of saying that everything we consume and produce affects the environment. When you toss a plastic bottle on the ground or leave the lights on all day, you contribute to pollution and waste precious natural resources. Being environmentally responsible means making conscious choices to reduce your negative impact. It starts with small, everyday habits: sorting your trash properly, using less plastic, carrying a reusable water bottle instead of buying and discarding disposable ones, and turning off lights when you leave a room. These simple actions may seem minor, but collectively, they make a huge difference in protecting the planet. Think about transportation, too. Whenever possible, opt for walking or cycling instead of driving. Public transport is another great alternative, as fewer cars on the road mean less pollution and cleaner air for everyone. Plus, cycling keeps you fit—so it's a win-win!

The food you eat also plays a role in environmental sustainability. Choosing locally grown and seasonal foods reduces transportation emissions and supports local farmers. Another great initiative is participating in environmental clean-up events. Many communities organize litter-picking days in parks, beaches, and urban areas, helping to keep public spaces clean and nature intact. Taking care of the environment isn't just a trend—it's a responsibility. Every small effort counts, and by making sustainable choices today, you help ensure a healthier planet for future generations.

90. Facing Emergencies

Emergencies are situations you hope to never experience, but knowing how to react can make the difference between total panic and effective action. Fires, earthquakes, car accidents—these events can happen when you least expect them, and being prepared can save lives. Take a fire, for example. The most important thing is to evacuate the building as quickly as possible. Never waste time trying to retrieve personal belongings—your life is far more valuable than your laptop or sneakers. Once you're safely outside, call the fire department immediately and avoid re-entering the building until it's declared safe.

Now, think of an earthquake. If you're indoors, don't run outside. Instead, take cover under a sturdy table or desk, staying away from windows and anything that could fall. Once the shaking stops, calmly exit the building, staying alert for debris and avoiding elevators. If you're involved in a car accident, the key is to stay calm. Check if you and others are injured, and call for help immediately if medical attention is needed. Never move an injured person unless absolutely necessary, as this could worsen their condition. One of the best ways to prepare for emergencies is to take a first-aid course, where you'll learn essential skills like applying bandages or performing CPR (Cardiopulmonary Resuscitation). Keeping a first-aid kit at home is also very important. Being prepared isn't about living in fear—it's about ensuring you're ready to act when it truly matters.

Chapter 10: 10 Mysteries About Your Parents

Welcome to the final chapter of this book, where we tackle one of the most complex and, at times, frustrating topics in a teenager's life: parents. Yes, those people who seem to have an innate talent for embarrassing you, saying things that make you roll your eyes, and setting rules that make no sense (at least to you). But—surprise!—your parents are also essential to your development and well-being. They may not always get things right, but most of what they do is meant to help you, even if it doesn't seem that way at first. This chapter is designed to help you understand your parents better and improve your relationship with them. You might not always agree with them, and they might not always understand you, but learning to communicate with them and seeing things from their perspective can make life at home much easier.

91. Why Do Your Parents Bother You?

Ever wonder why your parents seem to have a radar that lets them know exactly when you're about to do something fun and then cut you off? Or why they always insist on asking about your day, your grades, or who you're hanging out with? It might feel like they're on a mission to annoy you, but—believe it or not—there's actually a reason behind it.

First of all, your parents bother you because they love you. I know, I know, that sounds like a lame excuse, but it's the truth. They've spent years taking care of you, worrying about your health, your education, and your well-being. Now that you're growing up, they want to make sure you're heading in the right direction. Think of them like a coach—sometimes they push you hard or seem strict, but it's because they want to see you succeed. And here's another shocker: your parents were once teenagers too (yes, really!). They made mistakes, took bad advice, and learned the hard way. If they seem overprotective or overly involved, it's often because they don't want you to make the same mistakes they did. Another reason your parents can be annoying is that they see the world differently than you do. They've lived longer, so they know about dangers and opportunities you might not notice. So when they warn you about something, it's not just paranoia—it's experience. They've seen situations where things seemed innocent at first but later went terribly wrong. And yes, sometimes they annoy you simply because they're stressed too. Between work, bills, and a ton of responsibilities, being an adult isn't as easy as it seems. So when they ask you to do something or give you unsolicited advice, try to remember that they're human too. And who knows? One day, you might even realize they were right!

92. Understanding Your Parents' Point of View

Understanding your parents' point of view can feel like trying to crack an impossible code. But trust me, putting yourself in their shoes can make your relationship with them much easier. First of all, remember that your parents grew up in a completely different era. They didn't have TikTok, Instagram, or Fortnite. Their teenage experiences were nothing like yours, and that shapes how they see the world. If they don't understand why you spend hours online or why certain memes are funny, it's because their world was different. Instead of getting frustrated, try explaining your interests to them—it might help bridge the generation gap.

Another thing to keep in mind is that parents have a lot on their plate. Between work, bills, house maintenance, and maybe even health concerns (their own or other family members'), they carry a lot of stress. If they sometimes seem irritated or distracted, it's not necessarily because of you—they're just dealing with a ton of responsibilities. Understanding that can help you not take it personally when they seem overwhelmed. And here's a big one: your parents are not superheroes. They have insecurities, fears, and flaws just like you do. They make mistakes, sometimes unfair decisions, and they don't always get things right. Accepting that they are human—just like you—can help you be more patient with them. Instead of just clashing with them, try talking to them and asking why they think the way they do. You might be surprised to find out that their rules and concerns actually have reasons behind them. And when you show interest in their point of view, they're more likely to respect yours. At the end of the day, remember that your parents love you and genuinely want what's best for you. Even when they seem strict or unreasonable, their goal is to protect and guide you. Understanding their perspective doesn't mean you have to agree with them all the time, but it can help you see things from a different angle and find a middle ground.

93. How to Communicate with Your Parents

Talking to your parents can sometimes feel like trying to communicate in two completely different languages—without subtitles. But don't worry, there are ways to make communication smoother and avoid unnecessary conflicts. First, pick the right moment. Trying to have a serious conversation when your parents are stressed, tired, or busy is a bad idea. Instead, wait for a calm moment—maybe during dinner, on a walk, or when you're both relaxed. Calm moments lead to better discussions. Be clear and direct. Your parents can't read your mind (even though it sometimes seems like they can). If you have a problem or a request, explain it in a straightforward way. Instead of saying, "You never listen to me," try, "I feel like you don't understand what I'm saying about this, can we talk about it?" A clear explanation is always better than vague complaints.

When your parents talk, actually listen. Don't just think about how you're going to respond while they're speaking. Try to understand their point of view before reacting. Most importantly, don't be afraid to express your feelings. Your parents will appreciate you opening up to them, and it will help them understand you better. The more honest and respectful your conversations are, the easier it will be to build a strong and trusting relationship.

94. Conflicts and Disagreements

Conflicts and disagreements with your parents are inevitable, but they don't have to turn into endless battles. Learning to handle them with maturity can actually strengthen your relationship. When you feel like an argument is about to start, try to stay calm. I know, easier said than done—especially when you feel misunderstood or frustrated. But yelling or getting angry doesn't help. Take a deep breath and speak in a calm tone.

As I mentioned earlier, express yourself clearly and honestly. Instead of saying, "You never let me do anything!", try something like, "I feel frustrated because I'd like to have more freedom to decide how I spend my free time." This way, you're expressing your feelings without attacking your parents, which helps avoid unnecessary conflict. But don't just talk—listen to their reasons, too. Try to understand their opinions and look for a compromise. You won't always get exactly what you want, but often, there's a middle ground. For example, if you want to go out late but your parents are worried, you could agree to check in with them by message or come home slightly earlier. Small compromises can make a big difference in keeping peace while still gaining more freedom.

95. Learning from Your Parents

Your parents have a wealth of experience that can genuinely enrich your life. Sure, their "back in my day…" stories might sometimes make them sound like they're from another planet, but if you listen carefully, you might actually learn something useful. They've already gone through many of the same situations you're facing today. They've made mistakes, taken wrong turns, and learned valuable lessons along the way. Learning from their experiences can help you avoid making the same errors, saving you time and trouble. Beyond life lessons, your parents often have practical skills that can be incredibly handy. Maybe your dad knows how to change a tire in five minutes, or your mom can whip up an amazing meal with just a few ingredients. These skills aren't just convenient—they can save you money and make you more independent. And let's be honest, knowing how to cook something decent without relying on takeout is a life skill worth having. Their professional and social experiences can also be instructive. They can offer advice on how to deal with teachers, classmates, or different personalities in general. When it comes to friendships and relationships, they've been through heartbreak, arguments, and life lessons that could help you navigate your own challenges. Talking to them about these things might give you a new perspective.

Learning from your parents doesn't mean blindly following everything they say. It means listening, taking what's useful, and adapting it to your own life. You won't always agree with them, and that's perfectly normal.

But acknowledging that they've lived through experiences that could benefit you is a step toward maturity. So, the next time your parents start telling one of their "when I was your age…" stories, resist the urge to roll your eyes—you might actually pick up something valuable.

96. Celebrating Success Together

Imagine getting a great grade on a test or scoring the winning goal in a volleyball match. Sharing these achievements with your parents isn't just about showing them your progress—it's also about letting them take part in your victories. And believe it or not, as distant or strict as they might sometimes seem, your parents feel a deep sense of pride when they see you accomplish something that makes you happy.

By celebrating your successes with them, you also acknowledge their support. You might not always notice it, but behind every small victory, there's likely been a lot of effort on their part—helping you study late at night, driving you to practice, or simply encouraging you when things got tough. Recognizing their contribution makes them feel appreciated, which strengthens your bond and makes future challenges easier to face together. And don't think celebrations have to be anything extravagant. A simple family dinner, going out for ice cream, or watching a movie together can be a great way to mark the occasion. What truly matters is the shared moment. Plus, let's be honest—there's nothing wrong with taking a little time to brag about your achievements (as long as you don't overdo it, of course!).

97. Spending Time Together

Spending time with your parents doesn't have to feel like a boring routine—it can actually be fun if you find shared activities that bring you together. Instead of seeing family time as something forced, think of it as an opportunity to create meaningful memories. Start by identifying common interests. If you all enjoy nature, you could plan hiking or biking trips. Not only will you get fresh air and exercise, but these outings give you time to talk and bond without distractions. If sports are your thing, why not play a match together or follow a team you all like?

Cooking together is another great idea. Not only will you pick up new skills in the kitchen (and hopefully avoid setting anything on fire), but food always brings people closer. If one of your parents has a special hobby—gardening, fishing, model making, or even photography—ask them to teach you. Showing interest in their passions makes them feel valued and strengthens your connection. Even small activities, like watching a TV series together, playing board games, or taking a walk, can turn everyday moments into something special. The important thing is to find ways to share time together in a way that feels enjoyable for both of you.

98. Parents' Separation

Dealing with your parents' separation can feel like an emotional roller-coaster. But one thing you need to understand right away: it's not your fault. The reasons behind their decision are complex and involve only them, even if it affects you directly. You might wonder if you could have done something differently to prevent it, but the truth is, relationships are complicated—sometimes, despite all efforts, they just don't work out. It's completely normal to feel sad, angry, or confused. You might feel like your whole world has been turned upside down, but one thing remains unchanged: both of your parents still love you. Even if they now live in different homes, their affection for you doesn't diminish. Their separation might change some aspects of your daily life, but it doesn't change who you are or define your future.

Try to talk about how you're feeling with someone you trust—a friend, a teacher, or even a school counselor. Bottling up your emotions will only make things harder. Expressing your feelings helps you process them. And even though it may not seem like it now, this experience can teach you a lot about coping with change and becoming stronger as a person. It's a tough situation, but you will get through it.

99. Handling Criticism Constructively

Receiving criticism is never pleasant. Your first instinct might be to get defensive or dismiss it altogether, but not all criticism is meant to attack you. Often, your parents criticize you because they want to help you improve. Try to see their words as constructive feedback rather than judgment. It's like a volleyball coach telling you how to improve your spike—not because you're bad, but because they see potential in you and want you to succeed. When your parents criticize you, take a deep breath and really listen. Try to understand their point of view instead of immediately shutting down. If you're unsure about what they mean, ask for clarification—this shows that you're open to learning and growth. Handling criticism well is a skill that takes practice, but over time, you'll learn to turn feedback into a tool for self-improvement instead of taking it personally. Being able to accept and use criticism to your advantage will help you in every aspect of life, not just with your parents.

100. Family Traditions

Family traditions hold deep meaning and play a crucial role in strengthening bonds and creating lasting memories. They act like the glue that holds your family together, offering a sense of continuity and stability. Whether it's Sunday dinners, annual holiday celebrations, or simple habits like watching a movie together every Friday night, these rituals provide comfort and familiarity, especially when everything around you seems to be changing at lightning speed.

By actively participating in family traditions, you have the chance to create beautiful moments that will stay with you for the rest of your life. Think of the laughter, the inside jokes, and the special experiences you share on these occasions—one day, these will be the stories you tell your own children. Family traditions help you navigate tough times and make the happy moments even more meaningful. While they might sometimes feel like an obligation, try to see them for what they truly are: a sacred part of your family's identity, worth preserving and cherishing. And remember, traditions don't have to stay the same forever—you can create new ones! Maybe you can suggest a Sunday morning run in the park, a yearly road trip, or even a simple tradition like cooking a special meal together. Whatever it is, propose it, and your family just might follow!

Conclusion

We've reached the end of our journey through puberty—a ride full of ups and downs, discoveries, and challenges. But before we close this book, let's take a moment to reflect on what we've learned and how it can help you navigate this exciting (and sometimes tricky) phase of life.

First and foremost, puberty is a unique experience for every girl. There's no "right" time or way to grow up—each person develops at their own pace and in their own way. So, don't waste time comparing yourself to others—instead, focus on embracing your own journey.

Your physical, mental, and emotional health are incredibly important. Taking care of your body—eating well, exercising, and getting enough sleep—will not only make you feel better, but also help you manage stress and anxiety. And never forget: asking for help is not a weakness, but a sign of strength.

Sexuality is a natural part of growing up. Don't be afraid to explore and understand it, but always with respect for yourself and your partner. Healthy relationships—whether friendships or romantic ones—should be built on respect, communication, and trust.

School and learning aren't just about grades and homework. They're an opportunity to grow, discover new passions, and prepare for your future. Find a study method that works for you, develop your talents, and remember—learning never stops.

Addictions can sneak into many areas of life—from social media and shopping to alcohol and smoking. Being aware of these risks and knowing how to set boundaries will help you stay in control of your life.

The internet, social media, and technology offer endless opportunities, but they also come with serious risks. Use them wisely, protect your privacy, and remember—real life happens off-screen. Balancing online and offline time will help you build a happier, healthier, and more fulfilling life.

Becoming independent and responsible is a big step toward adulthood. Learning how to make decisions, develop practical skills, manage money, and respect the law will set you up for success. And don't forget—the world isn't just about you! Helping others and taking care of the planet are also part of becoming a strong, capable, and compassionate person.

Your relationship with your parents might feel complicated right now, but better communication and understanding their perspective can help a lot. They might not always get you, but they care about you more than you think.

If you enjoyed this book, I'd love for you to leave a review on Amazon—it only takes a few seconds but means the world to me! You can do so by scanning the following QR code with your smartphone:

If there's something you didn't like or think could be improved, please let me know by sending an email to m.pabst.en@booksgopublications.com. Your feedback will help make this book even better.

In the end, puberty and adolescence aren't just about change—they're also full of opportunities. Embrace these years with curiosity and courage, and never forget—you're not alone in this adventure. Wishing you an exciting and safe journey ahead!

Bibliography

1. **Breech, L., Holland-Hall, C., & Hewitt, G. (2005).** *The "well girl" exam.* Journal of Pediatric and Adolescent Gynecology, 18(4), 289-291.

2. **Fulton, J. E., Plewig, G., & Kligman, A. M. (1969).** *Effect of chocolate on acne vulgaris.* JAMA, 210(11), 2071-2074.

3. **Golden, N. H., Katzman, D., Kreipe, R., Stevens, S. L., Sawyer, S., Rees, J., Nicholls, D., & Rome, E. (2003).** *Eating disorders in adolescents: position paper of the Society for Adolescent Medicine.* The Journal of Adolescent Health, 33(6), 496-503.

4. **Hökby, S., Hadlaczky, G., Westerlund, J., Wasserman, D., Balázs, J., Germanavicius, A., Machín, N., Meszaros, G., Sarchiapone, M., Värnik, A., Varnik, P., Westerlund, M., & Carli, V. (2016).** *Are Mental Health Effects of Internet Use Attributable to the Web-Based Content or Perceived Consequences of Usage? A Longitudinal Study of European Adolescents.* JMIR Mental Health, 3.

5. **Paruthi, S., Brooks, L., D'Ambrosio, C., Hall, W., Kotagal, S., Lloyd, R. M., Malow, B., Maski, K., Nichols, C., Quan, S., Rosen, C., Troester, M., & Wise, M. (2016).** *Consensus Statement of the American Academy of Sleep Medicine on the Recommended Amount of Sleep for Healthy Children: Methodology and Discussion.* Journal of Clinical Sleep Medicine: JCSM, 12(11), 1549-1561.

6. **Pazarlis, P., Katsigiannopoulos, K., Papazisis, G., Bolimou, S., & Garyfallos, G. (2008).** *Compulsive buying: a review.* Annals of General Psychiatry, 7(1).

7. **Pearson, D., & Craig, T. (2014).** *The great outdoors? Exploring the mental health benefits of natural environments.* Frontiers in Psychology, 5.

8. **Rajanala, S., Maymone, M., & Vashi, N. (2018).** *Selfies-Living in the Era of Filtered Photographs.* JAMA Facial Plastic Surgery, 20(6), 443-444.

9. **Steptoe, A., & Butler, N. (1996).** *Sports participation and emotional wellbeing in adolescents.* The Lancet, 347, 1789-1792.

10. **Vingilyte, J., & Khadaroo, A. (2022).** *Personal clothing style and self-concept: Embracing the true, the ideal and the creative self.* Fashion, Style & Popular Culture.

11. **Wheeler, M. (1991).** *Physical changes of puberty.* Endocrinology and Metabolism Clinics of North America, 20(1), 1-14.

12. **Wise, R., & Robble, M. A. (2020).** *Dopamine and Addiction.* Annual Review of Psychology, 71, 79-106.

13. **Zimmer, F., & Imhoff, R. (2020).** *Abstinence from Masturbation and Hypersexuality.* Archives of Sexual Behavior, 49, 1333-1343.

Made in United States
North Haven, CT
29 May 2025

69339212R10061